Numerology

Spiritual Meaning of Numbers Including

(Reveal the Secret Power of Numbers and Discover How Numerological Divination is Connected to Astrology)

Michael Beasley

Published By **Phil Dawson**

Michael Beasley

All Rights Reserved

Numerology: Spiritual Meaning of Numbers Including (Reveal the Secret Power of Numbers and Discover How Numerological Divination is Connected to Astrology)

ISBN 978-1-7771996-3-0

No part of this guidebook shall be reproduced in any form without permission in writing from the publisher except in the case of brief quotations embodied in critical articles or reviews.

Legal & Disclaimer

The information contained in this book is not designed to replace or take the place of any form of medicine or professional medical advice. The information in this book has been provided for educational & entertainment purposes only.

The information contained in this book has been compiled from sources deemed reliable, and it is accurate to the best of the Author's knowledge; however, the Author cannot guarantee its accuracy and validity and cannot be held liable for any errors or omissions. Changes are periodically made to this book. You must consult your doctor or get professional medical advice before using any of the suggested remedies, techniques, or information in this book.

Upon using the information contained in this book, you agree to hold harmless the Author from and against any damages, costs, and expenses, including any legal fees potentially resulting from the application of any of the information provided by this guide. This disclaimer applies to any damages or injury caused by the use and application, whether directly or indirectly, of any advice or information presented, whether for breach of contract, tort, negligence, personal injury, criminal intent, or under any other cause of action.

You agree to accept all risks of using the information presented inside this book. You need to consult a professional medical practitioner in order to ensure you are both able and healthy enough to participate in this program.

Table Of Contents

Chapter 1: The Basics Of Numerology 1

Chapter 2: Calculating Your Numbers 35

Chapter 3: The Meanings Of The Numbers 53

Chapter 4: Numerology And Relationships 60

Chapter 5: Numerology And Career 78

Chapter 6: Advanced Numerology 90

Chapter 7: Using Numerology In Your Daily Life 105

Chapter 8: The Science Of Finding Your True Potential And Your Life Mission ... 117

Chapter 9: "The Universal Truth Of Numbers 145

Chapter 10: Discover Who You Are Purported To Be A Step-Thru-Step Guide. 181

Chapter 1: The Basics Of Numerology

The numbers 1-9

Number 1:

In numerology, the primary is taken into consideration a effective and independent good sized variety with a robust masculine electricity. It is related to leadership, new beginnings, creativity, and individuality.

People who have a existence route kind of one are frequently visible as confident and assertive. They have a sturdy feel of self and are driven to be successful. They are often natural leaders who're comfortable taking risks and making alternatives. They also are revolutionary and revolutionary, with a records for arising with new mind and answers.

The number 1 is likewise related to new beginnings and easy starts offevolved. It represents the begin of a modern-day day cycle and the functionality for growth and trade. People with a lifestyles course kind of one are frequently stimulated to make changes in their lives and pursue their goals and pursuits.

In relationships, the primary is related to independence and self-sufficiency. People with a existence path quantity of one may battle with compromise and can select to pursue their private pastimes in place of collaborating with others. However, they may be additionally reliable and dedicated to the ones they care approximately.

The primary is likewise related to creativity and self-expression. People with a life course massive variety of 1 also can have a information for the humanities or can be inquisitive about progressive pursuits together with writing, song, or artwork.

Overall, the number one is visible as a great and powerful range in numerology. It represents individuality, creativity, management, and the capacity for increase and change. People with a existence path variety of one are often pushed to be successful and are herbal leaders who're cushty taking dangers and pursuing their goals.

Number 2:

In numerology, the range 2 is often related to stability, harmony, and partnership. It is a girl amount, representing receptive energy and the trends of nurturing, compassion, and cooperation.

People with a life direction kind of are often visible as diplomatic and supportive. They have a sturdy choice to create concord and stability of their relationships and may have a skills for mediating conflicts. They are also empathetic and worrying, with a herbal ability to apprehend the emotions of others.

The quantity 2 is associated with the concept of partnership and collaboration. People with a life path variety of two may also additionally thrive in situations in which they may paintings carefully with others and make a contribution to a shared goal. They may also be interested in careers in fields which consist of counseling, social paintings, or schooling.

In relationships, the range 2 is associated with the trends of sensitivity and emotional intelligence. People with a life course sort of two can be quite attuned to the desires and emotions in their companions, and can prioritize the nicely-being in their relationships above their very non-public individual dreams.

The range 2 is also associated with creativity and instinct. People with a lifestyles course style of may additionally have a skills for the arts or may be interested by progressive pursuits collectively with writing or music. They might also furthermore have a robust revel in of intuition and be able to pick out out up on diffused cues and signals of their environment.

Overall, the variety 2 is seen as a harmonious and supportive variety in numerology. It represents the tendencies of stability, partnership, sensitivity, and creativity. People with a existence path quantity of two can be inquisitive about careers that comprise collaboration and may prioritize the properly-being of their relationships above their very personal man or woman dreams.

Number three:

In numerology, the range 3 is related to creativity, self-expression, and social connection. It is often seen as a lucky wide range, and is associated with optimism, enthusiasm, and a excessive quality outlook on lifestyles.

People with a existence path big sort of three are often seen as modern and expressive. They may have a expertise for the arts or can also experience sports activities collectively with writing, appearing, or music. They are frequently outgoing and sociable, with a natural capacity to connect to others and make buddies without problems.

The extensive range 3 is also associated with the idea of verbal exchange. People with a existence path form of 3 can also additionally have a skills for public talking or can be interested in careers in fields collectively with journalism, marketing and advertising, or marketing. They will also be expert at navigating social conditions and may have a talents for mediation and warfare decision.

In relationships, the amount three is related to the trends of heat and affection. People with a existence route type of three can be very expressive in their relationships and may prioritize spending time with loved ones.

The variety three is also related to the idea of growth and increase. People with a lifestyles path amount of three may be drawn to possibilities for non-public boom and may be interested by reading new skills or taking up new worrying situations.

Overall, the variety three is seen as a awesome and dynamic amount in numerology. It represents the tendencies of creativity, self-expression, verbal exchange, and social connection. People with a lifestyles path sort of three may additionally moreover moreover have a know-how for the arts or communication, and might prioritize spending time with cherished ones even as furthermore pursuing possibilities for private boom and improvement.

Number four:

In numerology, the variety 4 is associated with balance, safety, and practicality. It represents a sturdy foundation and a sturdy paintings ethic, and is frequently associated with the features of company, duty, and place.

People with a lifestyles path amount of four are frequently visible as dependable and reliable. They have a strong sense of duty and responsibility and are often dedicated to their work and their desires. They also can be expert at coping with projects and assets, and can have a expertise for planning and employer.

The quantity 4 is also related to the idea of stability and protection. People with a life route type of four may additionally prioritize financial stability and can be drawn to careers in fields which includes finance, accounting, or actual property.

In relationships, the variety four is related to the functions of loyalty and dedication. People with a existence route variety of 4 may be very reliable to their companions and might prioritize building a strong and steady domestic life.

The variety 4 is likewise related to the concept of order and form. People with a lifestyles route amount of four can be interested in structures and strategies, and can enjoy creating order out of chaos.

Overall, the variety 4 is seen as a stable and practical range in numerology. It represents the characteristics of stability, safety, responsibility, and place. People with a existence direction amount of 4 may prioritize building a solid and consistent lifestyles, and may be expert at managing assets and growing order out of chaos. They can also be loyal and committed companions who prioritize building a sturdy and solid home lifestyles.

Number five:

In numerology, the amount five is related to alternate, freedom, and journey. It represents a spirit of exploration and the pursuit of recent studies and opportunities.

People with a existence path massive type of five are often seen as adaptable and bendy. They may also have a understanding for navigating exchange and can be cushty with taking risks and trying new subjects. They can also be interested by careers in fields collectively with excursion, journalism, or entrepreneurship.

The variety five is likewise related to the concept of freedom and independence. People with a lifestyles route type of 5 may additionally prioritize their very own individual dreams and can resist being tied down by means of manner of obligations or commitments.

In relationships, the range 5 is related to the traits of pleasure and journey. People with a existence course kind of five can be interested in partners who proportion their love of exploration and might prioritize experiencing new topics together.

The quantity five is also associated with the idea of increase and evolution. People with a existence path big shape of five can be interested by private improvement and can be interested in opportunities for self-development and studying.

Overall, the large variety 5 is seen as a dynamic and adventurous amount in numerology. It represents the characteristics of trade, freedom, and exploration. People with a existence route variety of five may additionally prioritize their very own individual dreams and can be comfortable with taking dangers and attempting new matters. They may also be interested in careers and relationships that provide possibilities for boom and evolution.

Number 6:

In numerology, the range 6 is related to harmony, stability, and nurturing. It represents the idea of creating a experience of peace and concord in a unmarried's environment and with the ones round them.

People with a life route quantity of 6 are regularly visible as being concerned and nurturing. They can also additionally furthermore have a herbal abilities for growing a warm and alluring home environment, and can be interested in careers in fields which embody coaching, counseling, or healthcare.

The variety 6 is also associated with the concept of stability and concord. People with a existence path wide fashion of 6 also can prioritize growing a revel in of stability in their very very own lives and may be interested in possibilities for self-care and self-improvement.

In relationsnips, the variety 6 is associated with the functions of love and compassion. People with a life path quantity of 6 can also prioritize developing a loving and supportive home lifestyles, and may be very dedicated to their partners and circle of relatives.

The variety 6 is likewise related to the idea of provider and responsibility. People with a life course variety of 6 can be drawn to possibilities to help others and might enjoy a experience of duty to make a excellent effect on their community.

Overall, the big range 6 is seen as a nurturing and being involved quantity in numerology. It represents the characteristics of concord, balance, and compassion. People with a life path massive sort of 6 may also additionally furthermore prioritize growing a warm temperature and alluring home surroundings and can be drawn to careers and relationships that allow them to assist others and make a fine impact on their network. They can also prioritize their very private self-care and private boom if you need to create a experience of balance in their private lives.

Number 7:

In numerology, the sizeable range 7 is associated with introspection, spirituality, and intellectualism. It represents a deep desire to apprehend the world spherical us and to are searching for answers to life's large questions.

People with a existence route amount of seven are regularly seen as analytical and introspective. They can also have a natural expertise for crucial wondering and can be attracted to careers in fields along side generation, philosophy, or studies.

The extensive variety 7 is likewise associated with the idea of spirituality and the pursuit of deeper this means that. People with a life course range of 7 can be drawn to practices along with meditation, yoga, or prayer with a view to connect with a higher electricity or advantage a deeper information of themselves and the area round them.

In relationships, the variety 7 is related to the developments of depth and records. People with a lifestyles course variety of 7 might also furthermore prioritize deep and significant connections with their companions and might price highbrow and emotional compatibility over superficial tendencies.

The quantity 7 is likewise associated with the idea of independence and self-sufficiency. People with a existence direction range of seven may additionally additionally moreover prioritize their non-public inner adventure and may choose to spend time by myself an amazing manner to pursue their very own pursuits and introspection.

Overall, the huge variety 7 is visible as a deep and introspective quantity in numerology. It represents the traits of intellectualism, spirituality, and independence. People with a existence direction sizeable sort of seven may also prioritize their very personal internal journey and may be inquisitive about careers and relationships that allow them to pursue deeper which means that and expertise. They can also fee deep and sizable connections with others, however also can moreover prefer to spend time on my own at the manner to pursue their very very own pastimes and introspection.

Number eight:

In numerology, the range 8 is associated with ambition, success, and fabric wealth. It represents the concept of monetary abundance and achievement inside the fabric global.

People with a life path type of eight are regularly visible as bold and difficult-walking. They may have a herbal talents for business corporation and may be drawn to careers in fields which incorporates finance, actual property, or entrepreneurship.

The variety eight is also associated with the concept of private power and self-mastery. People with a life route form of eight may be pushed to reap success and economic abundance, but may additionally moreover prioritize private increase and self-improvement so that it will come to be their awesome selves.

In relationships, the variety eight is associated with the tendencies of loyalty and dependability. People with a lifestyles path sort of eight may furthermore prioritize balance and safety of their relationships, and may cost companions who percentage their ambition and stress for success.

The quantity eight is also related to the idea of karma and motive-and-impact. People with a lifestyles path amount of eight also can recollect within the concept that their actions have effects, and might try to make moral and accountable picks in all areas in their lives.

Overall, the variety 8 is seen as a powerful and bold amount in numerology. It represents the dispositions of success, wealth, and private power. People with a lifestyles course amount of eight can also prioritize sporting out economic abundance and can be interested in careers and opportunities that permit them to obtain their dreams. They also can moreover value balance and dependability of their relationships, and can try to make moral and accountable selections in all regions of their lives.

Number nine:

In numerology, the large range 9 is related to spirituality, humanitarianism, and ordinary love. It represents the concept very last contact and success, and is frequently seen as a effective and transformative big range.

People with a existence course huge sort of nine are frequently seen as compassionate and empathetic. They may also moreover have a strong preference to make a high first-rate distinction within the worldwide and can be interested by careers in fields inclusive of social paintings, counseling, or activism.

The massive range nine is also associated with the idea of spiritual enlightenment and the pursuit of better cognizance. People with a lifestyles route quantity of 9 can be interested in practices collectively with meditation, yoga, or mindfulness to be able to connect to their internal selves and the sector spherical them.

In relationships, the extensive variety nine is related to the abilities of empathy and compassion. People with a life path form of 9 also can furthermore prioritize know-how and reference to their companions, and can rate emotional and non secular compatibility over superficial trends.

The variety 9 is likewise related to the concept of selflessness and giving lower lower back to the network. People with a life direction type of 9 may additionally additionally experience a robust experience of responsibility to assist others and can be drawn to volunteer art work or activism at the manner to make a nice effect on the arena.

Overall, the range 9 is seen as a effective and transformative good sized range in numerology. It represents the tendencies of spirituality, humanitarianism, and normal love. People with a life route form of nine might also additionally prioritize developing a tremendous distinction within the worldwide and can be inquisitive about careers and possibilities that allow them to accumulate this motive. They may additionally moreover fee empathy and compassion of their relationships, and can feel a strong experience of responsibility to offer once more to the network and help others.

The Master numbers 11, 22, and 33

Master numbers are a special elegance of numbers in numerology that are taken into consideration to have a better vibration and a greater non secular importance than certainly one of a kind numbers. The 3 grasp numbers in numerology are 11, 22, and 33.

Master Number eleven:

Master range eleven is taken into consideration to be the maximum intuitive and spiritually aware of all the draw close numbers. It represents the functionality for non secular enlightenment and the ability to get proper of get admission to to better degrees of cognizance. People with a existence route quantity of 11 might also additionally have a heightened intuition and a robust connection to the non secular realm. They can be interested by spiritual practices collectively with meditation, yoga, or power recovery so that you can connect with their higher selves and the universe.

Master Number 22:

Master large variety 22 is often referred to as the "grasp builder" extensive variety, because it represents the capability for building and developing on a grand scale. People with a life course range of 22 may additionally have a natural skills for entrepreneurship, management, and company. They may be interested in careers in fields in conjunction with architecture, engineering, or business organization control. They may additionally additionally have a choice to make a powerful effect on the area thru their work.

Master Number 33:

Master variety 33 is regularly referred to as the "master instructor" large variety, because it represents the capability for religious management and steering. People with a life course amount of 33 also can have a natural competencies for coaching, mentoring, and galvanizing others. They can be drawn to careers in fields along with schooling, counseling, or religious leadership. They may additionally have a preference to make a immoderate satisfactory effect on the arena through their teachings and steerage.

Master numbers are taken into consideration to be a combination of the energies of their man or woman digits. For instance, the draw close big variety 11 is made from the energies of the number one and the huge range 2. The #1 represents individuality, independence, and management, while the huge range 2 represents intuition, balance, and concord. Together, the ones energies create a powerful aggregate that represents non secular enlightenment and intuition.

Similarly, the draw close variety 22 is made of the energies of the range 2 and the amount 4. The quantity 4 represents balance, commercial enterprise business enterprise, and practicality, even as the huge variety 2 represents intuition and stability. Together, the ones energies create a effective aggregate that represents the functionality for building and growing on a grand scale.

The preserve near variety 33 is made from the energies of the range three and the vast range 6. The variety three represents creativity, self-expression, and communique, at the same time as the range 6 represents concord, stability, and provider to others. Together, those energies create a effective combination that represents the ability for spiritual management and steering.

Overall, grasp numbers are taken into consideration to be an exquisite and powerful electricity in numerology. They constitute the capability for spiritual enlightenment, control, and creation or a grand scale. People with draw near numbers of their numerology chart can be inquisitive about careers and opportunities that allow them to unique their unique gadgets and make a splendid impact at the arena. They may additionally moreover additionally have a heightened intuition and a robust connection to the spiritual realm, and can be interested in non secular practices with a view to similarly increase their religious focus and capacity.

Life Path Number

In numerology, the life path number is taken into consideration to be the most essential range in an individual's numerology chart. It is calculated using someone's date of transport and represents the path that their existence is meant to take.

To calculate your life course amount, you want to function together the digits of your birthdate till you get a single digit variety. For instance, if your birthdate is March 25, 1990, you will upload three+2+5+1+9+nine+0 = 29, then upload 2+9 = eleven, that is a hold close range and does no longer want to be reduced in addition.

Each life course wide range has its personal particular because of this and represents considered one of a kind character traits, strengths, weaknesses, and life instructions. Here is a breakdown of every existence path extensive range and its corresponding developments:

Life Path Number 1:

People with a lifestyles course style of one are natural leaders who have a strong experience of independence, creativity, and ambition. They are self-inspired and characteristic a sturdy preference to achieve success. They will also be virtually impulsive and may be vulnerable to taking risks.

Life Path Number 2:

People with a life course sort of are natural peacemakers who've a sturdy experience of intuition, sensitivity, and global relations. They are high-quality at jogging with others and are regularly very cooperative and supportive. However, they may warfare with assertiveness and might will be inclined to keep away from warfare.

Life Path Number 3:

People with a lifestyles course form of 3 are cutting-edge and expressive human beings who have a robust revel in of satisfaction, optimism, and exuberance. They are often very social and enjoy being the center of interest. However, they may battle with strength of will and may have a propensity to procrastinate.

Life Path Number 4:

People with a lifestyles path sort of four are sensible and hardworking people who've a sturdy experience of challenge, agency, and interest to detail. They are often very reliable and reliable, but can also moreover warfare with expressing their emotions or taking dangers.

Life Path Number 5:

People with a existence route amount of five are adventurous and free-active human beings who have a robust enjoy of independence and a desire for alternate. They are regularly very adaptable and flexible, but can also struggle with committing to prolonged-time period plans or responsibilities.

Life Path Number 6:

People with a existence course number of 6 are nurturing and disturbing human beings who have a strong feel of responsibility and a choice to assist others. They are often very circle of relatives-orientated and rate relationships and partnerships. However, they may conflict with placing limitations and might end up overbearing or codependent.

Life Path Number 7:

People with a lifestyles course large variety of 7 are analytical and introspective human beings who've a robust experience of intuition and a desire for expertise and focus. They are regularly very religious and enjoy spending time by myself in mirrored image. However, they may battle with beginning as a whole lot as others and can end up too remoted or disconnected.

Life Path Number eight:

People with a existence path quantity of 8 are bold and motive-oriented people who have a robust revel in of electricity, authority, and economic achievement. They are frequently very employer-minded and excel at management and manage. However, they'll warfare with balancing their art work and private lives and might emerge as overly focused on fabric fulfillment.

Life Path Number nine:

People with a existence path large sort of 9 are compassionate and humanitarian people who have a strong feel of empathy and a desire to make a extraordinary impact on the arena. They are often very progressive and revel in working in fields together with the humanities, social paintings, or activism. However, they may conflict with letting bypass of the past and can turn out to be overly self-sacrificing or martyr-like.

Overall, the lifestyles route large variety can provide belief into an character

Expression Number

In numerology, the expression quantity is calculated using a person's full name and is assumed to represent their herbal competencies, capabilities, and person tendencies. It is also known as the future variety or the persona variety.

To calculate your expression variety, assign every letter to your whole name a numerical charge the use of tne chart under:

1: A, J, S

2: B, K, T

three: C, L, U

4: D, M, V

5: E, N, W

6: F, O, X

7: G, P, Y

eight: H, Q, Z

9: I, R

Then, upload collectively the numerical values for every letter for your name and decrease to a single digit range, until you switch out to be with a draw close range (eleven, 22, or 33), in which case you ll go away it as is.

Here are some examples of the way to calculate expression numbers:

John Smith

J=1, O=6, H=eight, N=5

S=1, M=4, I=nine, T=2, H=8

1+6+8+5+1+four+9+2+eight = forty four (master range)

Samantha Lee

S=1, A=1, M=4, A=1, N=5, T=2, H=eight, A=1

L=3, E=5, E=5

1+1+4+1+5+2+8+1+3+5+5 = 36 (master range)

Michael Jordan

M=four, I=nine, C=three, H=8, A=1, E=five, L=three

J=1, O=6, R=nine, D=four, A=1, N=five

four+9+3+eight+1+five+three+1+6+9+four+1+five = fifty 8 (five+8 = 13, reduces to four)

Once you have calculated your expression range, you may speak with the subsequent descriptions to gain belief into your person tendencies and capacity:

Expression Number 1:

People with an expression quantity of one are herbal leaders who are bold, independent, and assured. They are regularly very pushed and revel in taking over new worrying situations. They may additionally furthermore will be inclined to be stubborn or controlling.

Expression Number 2:

People with an expression variety of are cooperative, diplomatic, and intuitive. They are often very touchy to the emotions of others and excel at operating in partnership with others. They may also war with making selections or putting forward themselves.

Expression Number 3:

People with an expression massive kind of three are innovative, expressive, and constructive. They are frequently very social and enjoy being the center of interest. They also can conflict with strength of will or becoming overly scattered.

Expression Number four:

People with an expression amount of 4 are realistic, prepared, and reliable. They are regularly very hardworking and excel at building structures or structures. They may additionally additionally moreover struggle with expressing their emotions or taking risks.

Expression Number 5:

People with an expression huge fashion of five are adventurous, bendy, and unbiased. They are regularly very adaptable and enjoy taking on new opinions. They can also battle with committing to long-time period plans or duties.

Expression Number 6:

People with an expression huge style of 6 are nurturing, being involved, and family-orientated. They are regularly very responsible and excel at developing harmonious relationships. They may additionally battle with placing obstacles or turning into overly controlling.

Expression Number 7:

People with an expression quantity of 7 are introspective, analytical, and religious. They are regularly very highbrow and revel in exploring deep topics or philosophical questions. They may additionally additionally additionally will be inclined to be reserved or introverted. Those with this expression large variety might also additionally have a herbal knowledge for studies or assessment and are often attracted to careers in era or academia. They can also moreover have a robust hobby in spirituality or metaphysics.

Expression Number eight:

People with an expression quantity of eight are formidable, practical, and employer-minded. They are often very focused on attaining fulfillment and can be inquisitive about careers in finance, law, or entrepreneurship. They have a herbal information for leadership and can be very professional at dealing with humans or belongings. Those with this expression variety can also battle with locating stability of their paintings and personal life, and can need to domesticate self-reputation and mindfulness to keep away from burnout.

Expression Number nine:

People with an expression wide kind of 9 are compassionate, humanitarian, and idealistic. They are frequently very concerned with making the sector a higher vicinity and may be interested in careers in social justice or philanthropy. They have a natural know-how for empathy and may be very professional at connecting with others on an emotional degree. Those with this expression quantity can also warfare with perfectionism or becoming overly related to their ideals, and may need to exercise self-care and self-recognition to keep away from burnout or disillusionment. They are often seen as clever and intuitive, and may be drawn to non secular or restoration practices.

Soul Urge Number

The Soul Urge Number, also called the Heart's Desire Number, is one of the middle numbers in numerology that gives notion into someone's innermost goals, motivations, and aspirations. This quantity is derived from the vowels in a person's complete starting name and can offer precious records about someone's personality, values, and emotional inclinations.

To calculate the Soul Urge Number, one want to assign a numerical fee to every vowel in someone's complete shipping call the usage of the following chart:

A, E, I, O, U = 1

Y = 7

For example, if a person's whole delivery call is Sarah Elizabeth Smith, the vowels in her name may be A, E, E, I, E, and O. Assigning a numerical rate to each vowel and including them collectively, we get:

1 + five + 5 + nine + 5 + 6 = 31

Since the Soul Urge Number is a single-digit range, we then add the digits together till we get a single-digit result:

3 + 1 = 4

Therefore, Sarah Elizabeth Smith's Soul Urge Number would be four.

Here's a breakdown of what each Soul Urge Number represents:

Soul Urge Number 1: People with this huge range are pushed, bold, and determined. They have a robust choice for achievement and manage and might warfare with emotions of inadequacy or fear of failure.

Chapter 2: Calculating Your Numbers

Step-with the useful resource of-step manual to calculating your Life Path Number

Calculating your Life Path Number in numerology is a straightforward method that consists of together with up the digits in your date of begin until you get a single-digit variety. This amount is a powerful indicator of your life's purpose, annoying conditions, and opportunities, and might provide valuable perception into your character and destiny.

Here's a step-through-step guide to calculating your Life Path Number:

Step 1: Write down your complete date of start

Write down your whole date of delivery in numerical form (MM/DD/YYYY). For instance, when you have been born on January 1st, 1990, your date of delivery might be 01/01/1990.

Step 2: Reduce the month, day, and twelve months to unmarried digits

Reduce the month, day, and three hundred and sixty five days of your transport to unmarried digits. To do this, upload collectively the digits in every phase of your birthdate one after the alternative till you get a single-digit variety or a grasp large variety (11, 22, or 33). For instance:

Month: January is the number one month of the yr, so it's miles represented through way of the number one. Therefore, 01 turns into zero+1=1.

Day: The day of your beginning is represented through a number of from 1 to 31. If your birthday is January 1st, then the day vast range is 1. Therefore, 01 turns into 0+1=1.

Year: The yr of your starting is represented via way of 4 digits. For example, if you were born in 1990, the 3 hundred and sixty 5 days might be represented thru way of the numbers 1, 9, nine, and 0. Therefore, 1990 turns into 1+9+9+0=19, which can be similarly reduced to at least one+9=10, after which to at least one+zero=1.

Step three: Add the single-digit numbers collectively

Add the unmarried-digit numbers collectively to get your Life Path Number. If at any issue during the calculation you get a master variety (eleven, 22, or 33), you do no longer reduce it to a unmarried digit, as the ones numbers are considered effective and function their very private unique meanings.

For instance, the usage of the birthdate 01/01/1990:

Month: zero+1=1

Day: 0+1=1

Year: 1+nine+nine+0=19 (hold close amount)

Total: 1+1+19=21 (which may be in addition decreased to 2+1=3)

In this situation, the Life Path Number is 21/three, indicating that the person's lifestyles reason involves creativity, self-expression, and communication.

Calculating your Expression, Soul Urge, and Personality numbers

Calculating your expression considerable variety :

Calculating your expression variety is a sincere procedure in numerology. Your expression large variety is calculated using the numerical values assigned to the letters of your full begin name. This amount exhibits your natural capabilities, abilities, and potentials.

Here is a step-via-step manual on a manner to calculate your expression variety:

Step 1: Assign numerical values to each letter for your whole transport name

Each letter within the English alphabet has a corresponding numerical charge. You can use the following chart to assign numerical values to the letters to your call:

1 2 three four five 6 7 8 9

A B C D E F G H I

J K L M N O P Q R

S T U V W X Y Z

For instance, in case your complete shipping call is John Smith, you may assign the following numerical values:

JOHNSMITH

1+6+8+5+1+4+9+2+8 = forty four

Note: It is essential to apply your entire begin call to calculate your expression range because it ought to be. This includes your first, center, and final name.

Step 2: Reduce the sum to a single-digit variety or a draw close large range

If your sum is a -digit variety, you need to lessen it to a single-digit quantity or a master range. Master numbers are 11, 22, and 33, and they'll be not reduced to a unmarried digit.

For instance, in case your sum is forty 4, you may lessen it to eight thru at the side of 4+four=8.

Step 3: Interpret your expression massive range

Once you have calculated your expression variety, you can use it to apprehend your natural abilities, skills, and potentials.

Expression number one: People with this range are independent, bold, and progressive. They have robust management talents and are herbal entrepreneurs.

Expression range 2: People with this variety are diplomatic, empathetic, and cooperative. They are accurate at running with others and function a knowledge for mediation and global relations.

Expression variety three: People with this range are expressive, progressive, and social. They have a statistics for conversation, leisure, and the arts.

Expression range 4: People with this huge variety are sensible, disciplined, and hardworking. They have a abilities for commercial enterprise organization and manipulate.

Expression range 5: People with this quantity are adventurous, curious, and bendy. They have a skills for conversation, adventure, and entrepreneurship.

Expression extensive variety 6: People with this variety are nurturing, accountable, and loving.

They have a skills for schooling, counseling, and recovery.

Expression big variety 7: People with this quantity are analytical, introspective, and non secular. They have a know-how for studies, assessment, and philosophy.

Expression widespread variety eight: People with this range are formidable, successful, and materialistic. They have a skills for business enterprise, finance, and manipulate.

Expression number nine: People with this extensive variety are compassionate, current, and idealistic. They have a talents for philanthropy, social artwork, and the arts.

Calculating your soul urge massive variety :

Calculating your Soul Urge Number is a sincere technique that includes summing up the numerical values of the vowels to your complete beginning call. Here is a step-through way of the use of-step manual to calculating your Soul Urge Number:

Step 1: Write out your full transport name.

The first step in calculating your Soul Urge Number is to put in writing out your whole delivery name, which includes your middle name. Use the selection that appears to your beginning certificate, as it is the maximum correct instance of your call numerology.

Step 2: Assign numerical values to the vowels on your name.

Next, you want to assign numerical values to the vowels for your call. In numerology, each vowel is assigned a selected variety. Here is the numerical rate assigned to every vowel:

A = 1

E = 5

I = nine

O = 6

U = 3

For instance, in case your starting name is John William Smith, the vowels for your call is probably "o," "i," "i," and "a." Therefore, the numerical values assigned to the ones vowels might be 6, nine, nine, and 1.

Step 3: Add up the numerical values of the vowels.

Once you've got assigned numerical values to the vowels for your name, the following step is to characteristic up those values. For example, if the numerical values of the vowels on your name are 6, 9, 9, and 1, you will upload the ones numbers together to get a whole of 25.

Step 4: Reduce the sum to a unmarried-digit quantity.

Finally, you need to lessen the sum to a single-digit sizable range, that's your Soul Urge Number. If the sum is a double-digit variety, you may reduce it with the beneficial useful resource of such as the 2 digits collectively. For instance, if the sum of the numerical values of the vowels in your call is 25, you will upload 2 + 5 to get a complete of 7. Therefore, your Soul Urge Number is 7.

It's truely well worth noting that the letter "Y" may be both a vowel or a consonant, relying on wherein it appears on your call. If "Y" seems to your name as a vowel, meaning that it seems in a syllable and no longer using a distinct vowel, you need to assign it a numerical rate based mostly on its vowel sound. If "Y" appears for your name as a consonant, which means that it appears in a syllable with each unique vowel, you have to no longer include it to your calculation of your Soul Urge Number.

In stop, calculating your Soul Urge Number is a easy approach that includes assigning numerical values to the vowels on your start call and at the side of them as much as get a unmarried-digit quantity. Your Soul Urge Number can provide you with belief into your private dreams and motivations, and will will permit you to better apprehend your self and your life course.

Calculating your persona range :

Your Personality Number is an critical component of your numerology chart. It famous your precise person tendencies and traits that make you stand proud of others. The method of calculating your Personality Number involves assigning numerical values to the consonants on your whole begin call. Here is a step-with the useful resource of manner of-step guide to calculating your Personality Number:

Step 1: Write out your complete starting name.

The first step in calculating your Personality Number is to put in writing out your complete delivery call, such as your center call. Use the choice that looks to your beginning certificate, as it's miles the most correct illustration of your call numerology.

Step 2: Assign numerical values to the consonants in your call.

Next, you want to assign numerical values to the consonants in your call. In numerology, each consonant is assigned a selected range. Here is the numerical price assigned to each consonant:

B = 2

C = 3

D = four

F = 6

G = 7

H = eight

J = 1

K = 2

L = three

M = four

N = 5

P = 7

Q = eight

R = nine

S = 1

T = 2

V = four

W = 5

X = 6

Z = eight

For example, in case your delivery call is John William Smith, the consonants in your call might be "j," "h," "n," "w," "l," "m," "s," "t," and "h." Therefore, the numerical values assigned to the ones consonants can be 1, eight, 5, five, 3, 4, 1, 2, and 8.

Step three: Add up the numerical values of the consonants.

Once you have were given assigned numerical values to the consonants to your name, the following step is to add up those values. For example, if the numerical values of the consonants on your name are 1, 8, five, 5, three, four, 1, 2, and 8, you'll upload these numbers collectively to get a entire of 37.

Step four: Reduce the sum to a unmarried-digit amount.

Finally, you need to reduce the sum to a single-digit amount, that's your Personality Number. If the sum is a double-digit range, you may reduce it via manner of which includes the two digits together. For example, if the sum of the numerical values of the consonants on your name is 37, you'll upload three + 7 to get an entire of 10. Therefore, your Personality Number is 1.

It's in reality properly really worth noting which you ought to now not encompass vowels, "Y," or some other particular characters on your calculation of your Personality Number. Only consonants assume this tool.

Your Personality Number is an critical part of your numerology chart, as it is able to give you precious perception into your person and individual tendencies. It reveals the skills that you are acknowledged for, the unique tendencies that make you stand happy with others, and the components of your person that you can want to artwork on. Understanding your Personality Number assist you to gain a deeper knowledge of yourself and your relationships with others.

In quit, calculating your Personality Number is a clean manner that involves assigning numerical values to the consonants for your starting name and adding them as lots as get a single-digit quantity. Your Personality Number can offer you with valuable belief into your persona tendencies and tendencies, supporting you to better understand your self and people round you.

How to interpret your numbers

Numerology is the exercise of assigning numerical values to letters and the use of them to gain notion into an person's man or woman tendencies, lifestyles path, and unique components in their life. Once you have were given calculated your Life Path, Expression, Soul Urge, and Personality numbers, the subsequent step is to interpret them. Here is a step-with the aid of manner of-step manual at the manner to interpret your numbers:

Understand the meanings of the numbers

Each variety in numerology has its very own particular meaning and significance. It's critical to have a easy records of what each range represents earlier than deciphering your numbers. Here's a brief evaluation of the meanings of the numbers 1-nine and draw close numbers eleven, 22, and 33:

1: Leadership, independence, innovation, self-self guarantee

2: Diplomacy, cooperation, intuition, sensitivity

3: Creativity, self-expression, optimism, socialization

four: Organization, stability, tough paintings, practicality

5: Adaptability, freedom, journey, curiosity

6: Responsibility, nurturing, harmony, domesticity

7: Analysis, spirituality, introspection, knowledge

eight: Ambition, energy, success, wealth

9: Humanitarianism, compassion, of completion, idealism

11: Visionary, intuition, sensitivity, religious interest

22: Master builder, practicality, idealism, control

33: Master trainer, compassion, selflessness, idea

Look on the strengths and weaknesses related to every variety

Once you understand the overall because of this that of every variety, you could begin to have a study the strengths and weaknesses related to them. For example, someone with a Life Path type of 1 is probable to be a herbal chief and feature strong self-self perception, however can also conflict with being too controlling or stubborn at instances. Understanding the ones strengths and weaknesses assist you to better understand yourself and others.

Consider the have an impact on of draw close numbers

If you have a hold near quantity in any of your calculations (eleven, 22, or 33), it's miles essential to bear in mind their impact. Master numbers are considered to have a higher religious importance and can propose a strong functionality for growth and fulfillment, but can also come with stressful conditions and duties.

Look at the relationships among your numbers

Once you've got interpreted every of your numbers for my part, you could start to have a take a look at the relationships among them. For example, in case your Life Path range is 1 and your Expression range is 5, you can have a sturdy strength for management and independence, but furthermore a desire for journey and freedom. By know-how those relationships, you could advantage deeper insights into your person and existence path.

Consider the have an effect on of various factors

Chapter 3: The Meanings Of The Numbers

The significance of every range in Numerology

Numerology assigns importance to each amount from 1 to 9, similarly to to the grasp numbers eleven, 22, and 33. Each huge variety has its private specific energy and symbolism in numerology, which can be used to advantage belief into numerous factors of lifestyles, such as persona trends, strengths, weaknesses, and existence path.

Here are the significance of each range in numerology:

1: The number one represents independence, control, ambition, and creativity. It is associated with new beginnings and is regularly considered the most powerful variety in numerology. People with a life path sort of 1 are often assured, driven, and centered on their goals.

2: The significant range 2 represents balance, concord, partnership, and worldwide contributors of the circle of relatives. It is related to relationships and cooperation.

People with a life direction variety of are often touchy, empathetic, and intuitive.

3: The range three represents creativity, self-expression, and optimism. It is related to communication and social interplay. People with a lifestyles route form of three are regularly modern, outgoing, and enjoy expressing themselves thru various mediums.

four: The huge variety 4 represents balance, tough paintings, and practicality. It is related to company and form. People with a existence path variety of 4 are frequently dependable, realistic, and green.

5: The huge range five represents freedom, adventure, and trade. It is related to interest and pleasure. People with a lifestyles route amount of 5 are regularly flexible, adaptable, and enjoy exploring new critiques.

6: The range 6 represents love, nurturing, and compassion. It is associated with circle of relatives and community. People with a existence course huge type of 6 are frequently annoying, accountable, and experience helping others.

7: The variety 7 represents introspection, analysis, and spirituality. It is associated with inner knowledge and instinct. People with a lifestyles direction sort of 7 are often analytical, philosophical, anc revel in delving into the mysteries of lifestyles.

8: The quantity eight represents material success, energy, and abundance. It is associated with wealth and industrial enterprise. People with a life direction amount of eight are frequently ambitious, confident, and enjoy monetary achievement.

nine: The range 9 represents humanitarianism, compassior, and spirituality. It is associated with provider and helping others. People with a lifestyles directior large form of nine are regularly selfless, compassionate, and committed to developing a excessive pleasant distinction in the international.

eleven: The range 11 is a grasp amount that represents intuition, religious enlightenment, and divine perception. It is related to heightened psychic skills and spiritual awakening. People with a lifestyles path variety of 11 are frequently spiritually gifted, intuitive, and can have a calling to serve others.

22: The variety 22 is a draw near massive range that represents practicality, material mastery, and building a legacy. It is related to the capacity to show goals into fact and leave a long lasting impact on the place. People with a existence course sort of twenty-two are regularly visionary, formidable, and feature the ability for exquisite success.

33: The amount 33 is a draw close amount that represents creativity, nurturing, and selflessness. It is related to the functionality to encourage and uplift others. People with a life direction sort of 33 are frequently significantly superior souls, with a deep enjoy of compassion and the selection to make a excessive great effect on the sector.

Understanding the importance of each extensive range in numerology assist you to advantage belief into various factors of lifestyles, at the side of your personality tendencies, strengths, weaknesses, and life course. By reading to interpret the that means of numbers, you may advantage a deeper statistics of your self and the vicinity spherical you.

Positive and terrible additives of each amount

Numerology assigns powerful brilliant and negative trends to each huge variety. While those characteristics aren't absolute and may range counting on various factors in a person's numerology chart, they're capable of offer treasured perception into someone's strengths and weaknesses.

1: Positive traits encompass independence, management, and ambition, even as negative traits can encompass selfishness, aggression, and a tendency closer to isolation.

2: Positive trends encompass diplomacy, cooperation, and sensitivity, at the same time as terrible tendencies can include indecisiveness, dependency, and a lack of self-self assure.

three: Positive tendencies encompass creativity, optimism, and communication abilties, on the same time as poor trends can embody a loss of reputation, procrastination, and superficiality.

four: Positive dispositions embody reliability, field, and practicality, at the same time as poor tendencies can consist of stubbornness, stress, and an aversion to alternate.

five: Positive dispositions encompass versatility, adaptability, and a love of freedom, even as lousy developments can include restlessness, impulsiveness, and a lack of willpower.

6: Positive tendencies encompass nurturing, concord, and responsibility, at the same time as bad traits can encompass overprotectiveness, self-righteousness, and a unethical closer to martyrdom.

7: Positive dispositions encompass statistics, intuition, and highbrow interests, at the equal time as awful trends can embody aloofness, cynicism, and a dishonest within the direction of isolation.

eight: Positive developments encompass ambition, cloth achievement, and practicality, at the same time as horrible developments can consist of a lack of compassion, materialism, and a dishonest inside the course of domination.

nine: Positive tendencies encompass humanitarianism, empathy, and spirituality, while horrific inclinations can encompass martyrdom, self-righteousness, and a bent towards escapism.

Master Numbers:

eleven: Positive traits embody intuition, belief, and creativity, whilst bad traits can embody anxiety, indecisiveness, and an inclination closer to impracticality.

Chapter 4: Numerology And Relationships

Compatibility of Life Path Numbers

In numerology, Life Path Numbers are believed to hold big because of this and may display lots about a person's person, trends, and tendencies. Knowing your very private Life Path Number can offer valuable insights into your lifestyles and relationships, collectively with compatibility with others who percent the equal or considered one of a kind Life Path Numbers.

Here's a breakdown of compatibility for every Life Path Number:

1 and 1

When 1s come collectively, they may proportion a robust choice for independence and management. They are each ambitious and determined, and this could create a aggressive and from time to time hard dynamic. However, they can also useful resource each special's goals and proportion a powerful strain towards fulfillment.

1 and multiple

The 1's choice for independence can struggle with the two's want for harmony and compromise. However, if they are capable of discover a stability and paintings closer to commonplace goals, this partnership can be a hit. The 2 can deliver a feel of emotional intensity and nurturing to the relationship.

1 and three

The 1 and 3 may be a dynamic duo, as both percentage a love for self-expression and creativity. They can encourage every specific and art work nicely together in pursuing their passions. However, the 1 also can moreover need to apprehend of no longer dominating the relationship.

1 and 4

The 1 and 4 can complement each exceptional properly, with the 1's stress and ambition balanced with the aid of the four's practicality and stability. They can create a sturdy foundation collectively, however may additionally additionally moreover want to speak openly to avoid clashes of their technique to achieving their goals.

1 and five

The 1 and 5 can percentage a feel of adventure and exploration, however may additionally moreover conflict to discover not unusual ground beyond that. The 1's desire for manage can war with the five's need for freedom and spontaneity, making compromise and conversation critical for this pairing to gain success.

1 and six

The 1 and six can create a robust partnership, with the 1's energy and ambition complementing the 6's nurturing and loving nature. They can balance each other out well, however the 1 can also moreover need to be privy to not dominating the connection.

1 and seven

The 1 and 7 may additionally have particular strategies to lifestyles and might want to make an effort to understand each other's perspectives. The 7 may be greater introspective and spiritual, at the same time as the 1 is extra targeted on accomplishing success in the cloth global. However, if they're able to find out a balance, this partnership can be successful.

1 and 8

The 1 and 8 can create a powerful and a fulfillment partnership, with each sharing a power closer to success and financial stability. They can supplement each unique's strengths nicely, however can also furthermore want to talk brazenly to avoid clashes of their technique to reaching their desires.

1 and nine

The 1 and nine can percentage a choice to make a difference within the global, however may additionally have distinct strategies to accomplishing that reason. The 1 is targeted on personal success, while the 9 is targeted on humanitarian efforts. However, they might nonetheless create a a success partnership if they may be capable of discover a stability.

2 and multiple

When 2s come collectively, they're able to create a harmonious and nurturing partnership. They each cost emotional depth and connection, and might create a heat and loving surroundings for themselves and people spherical them.

2 and three

The 2 and 3 can supplement every other well, with the two's sensitivity and nurturing nature balanced via the 3's creativity and self-expression. They can inspire every notable and create a a laugh and dynamic dating.

2 and four

The 2 and four can create a strong and practical partnership, with the two's emotional intensity balanced with the aid of the four's practicality and reliability. They can aid each unique in professional lifestyles and private existence.

Expression Number and relationships

In numerology, the Expression Number is calculated based completely mostly on the total call given at shipping, representing the inherent capabilities, capabilities, and possibilities of an man or woman. The range ought to have a large impact on relationships and the manner one interacts with others. Here are some strategies that Expression Number can have an effect on relationships:

Expression Number 1:

Individuals with Expression Number 1 have a tendency to be independent and confident, frequently taking the lead in relationships. They are driven, formidable, and targeted on engaging in their dreams. This can every so often bring about a loss of sensitivity within the course of others, as they'll prioritize their private goals over the ones of their accomplice. However, they are furthermore very dependable and protecting of these they love.

Expression Number 2:

People with Expression Number 2 are sensitive and diplomatic, with a desire for concord of their relationships. They are herbal peacemakers and regularly placed the needs of others before their private. This can once in a while purpose an inclination to be taken benefit of in relationships, as they may prioritize their companion's desires over their personal. However, they'll be also loving and nurturing, with a deep functionality for empathy and compassion.

Expression Number three:

Individuals with Expression Number 3 tend to be revolutionary, expressive, and outgoing, with a tremendous sense of humor. They thrive in social situations and experience connecting with others. However, they also can be prone to temper swings and can struggle with self-doubt. In relationships, they will be very passionate and romantic, but may additionally additionally conflict with willpower and might prioritize their non-public freedom over the goals in their companion.

Expression Number four:

People with Expression Number four are sensible, dependable, and hardworking, with a strong enjoy of obligation and responsibility.

They will be inclined to fee balance and protection in their relationships, and may struggle with trade or uncertainty. However, they may be moreover very dependable and dedicated, with a deep sense of admire for culture and own family values.

Expression Number five:

Individuals with Expression Number five are adventurous, loose-spirited, and unconventional, with a desire for pride and range of their lives. They thrive on trade and can conflict with dedication or recurring. In relationships, they will prioritize their very personal independence over the goals in their partner, however additionally can be very passionate and romantic.

Expression Number 6:

People with Expression Number 6 are loving, nurturing, and deeply dedicated to their relationships. They charge concord and stability in their lives and can warfare with conflict or discord. However, in addition they'll be susceptible to being overbearing or controlling, as they will prioritize their own need for harmony over the desires of their partner.

Expression Number 7:

Individuals with Expression Number 7 are introspective, analytical, and spiritual, with a deep choice for statistics and knowledge. They will be predisposed to be unbiased and self-sufficient, and can conflict with emotional expression or intimacy. In relationships, they may be very loyal and committed, however can also moreover warfare with vulnerability and might prioritize their private need for solitude over the goals of their associate.

Expression Number 8:

People with Expression Number 8 are ambitious, effective, and pushed, with a robust preference for achievement and reputation. They will be predisposed to be confident and self-confident, but may additionally moreover warfare with emotional expression or vulnerability. In relationships, they may prioritize their very own goals for achievement over the dreams of their partner, but moreover can be very dependable and committed.

Expression Number nine:

Expression Number 9 is understood to be compassionate, empathetic, and idealistic, that could make them a remarkable partner in a dating. They have a propensity to be mainly intuitive and might resultseasily experience the emotions of others. However, their idealism and desire for perfection can once in a while cause them to be important in their companions, which may additionally additionally result in warfare in the relationship. Additionally, their robust enjoy of independence and want for personal area can also now and again be misinterpreted as aloofness or disinterest. Overall, Expression Number nine humans might also have a deep and considerable impact on their relationships if they are capable of balance their idealism with practicality and talk successfully with their partner.

Soul Urge Number and relationships

In numerology, the Soul Urge Number is notion to represent a person's innermost desires and motivations. It is calculated primarily based completely at the vowels in a person's call and may display lots approximately their persona and relationships. Here, we will find out the impact of Soul Urge Numbers 1-five on relationships.

Soul Urge Number 1

People with Soul Urge Number 1 are formidable, impartial, and self-reliant. They are pushed to be successful and can be specially competitive in relationships. They fee their freedom and can have a tough time compromising of their relationships. However, they may be passionate and committed partners within the event that they revel in professional and favored. Their partners should be prepared to guide their desires and supply them the distance they want to pursue their desires.

Soul Urge Number 2

People with Soul Urge Number 2 are kind, empathetic, and nurturing. They value harmony and cooperation of their relationships and can be surprisingly touchy to their associate's emotions. They can now and again be indecisive and can conflict to mention their personal needs within the relationship. They are most well matched with companions who can provide them with emotional guide and assist them feel solid.

Soul Urge Number three

People with Soul Urge Number 3 are progressive, expressive, and high first-rate. They are playful and a laugh-loving, and that they fee a associate who can percentage their sense of humor. They can once in a while be unpredictable and may battle with willpower of their relationships. They are most well matched with partners who can useful resource their innovative endeavors and appreciate their spontaneous nature.

Soul Urge Number 4

People with Soul Urge Number 4 are dependable, realistic, and hardworking. They charge stability and safety of their relationships and can be hesitant to take risks. They can sometimes be inflexible and may war to comply to alternate within the relationship. They are most properly matched with companions who percentage their values and might offer them with a enjoy of stability and ordinary.

Soul Urge Number five

People with Soul Urge Number 5 are adventurous, curious, and flexible. They fee freedom and can have a difficult time settling down in a long-time period courting. They may be impulsive and may conflict with determination in their relationships. They are most properly suitable with partners who can provide them with a feel of excitement and novelty and who can adapt to their converting hobbies and desires.

Soul Urge Number 6:

People with Soul Urge Number 6 are being concerned, nurturing, and protective humans.

They have a herbal inclination within the route of assisting others and are often attracted to those who need assist and help. In a dating, they will be predisposed to prioritize their companion's desires and are constantly equipped to make sacrifices to make certain their happiness. However, they can also be possessive and controlling, which could purpose conflicts within the courting.

Soul Urge Number 7:

People with Soul Urge Number 7 are introspective, analytical, and spiritual humans. They will be predisposed to preserve to themselves and fee their non-public region and independence. In a dating, they are looking for a deep connection and highbrow stimulation from their companion. However, additionally they'll be emotionally far off and aloof, which can be perceived as a lack of hobby or strength of will.

Soul Urge Number 8:

People with Soul Urge Number 8 are formidable, pushed, and purpose-orientated human beings. They prioritize their profession and financial balance over relationships, that might lead them to seem bloodless and detached. However, they're moreover dependable and dedicated companions who are searching for stability and safety in their relationships. They generally will be predisposed to draw partners who percentage similar values and desires.

Soul Urge Number 9:

People with Soul Urge Number nine are compassionate, generous, and humanitarian humans. They have a deep experience of empathy and are regularly interested in social motives and activism. In a dating, they prioritize emotional intimacy and connection, and are inclined to make sacrifices for their companion's happiness. However, they also can be idealistic and susceptible to self-sacrifice, which can motive them to overlook their very personal desires and goals.

Personality Number and relationships

In numerology, the personality amount is calculated the usage of the consonants in someone's entire name. It represents the outward look and character that an person duties to the area. It is idea to steer someone's behavior, thoughts-set, and the way they interact with others, including their romantic relationships. Let's discover the impact of person numbers 1 via 5 on relationships.

Personality Number 1: Individuals with this range will be inclined to be assertive, impartial, and driven. They are natural leaders who want to take fee and function a strong enjoy of self. In relationships, they will struggle with compromising or sharing manage, however they may be dependable and committed partners. Their companions want in order to receive their need for independence and admire their manage abilities.

Personality Number 2: People with this variety will be predisposed to be touchy, diplomatic, and nurturing. They are peacemakers who charge concord and cooperation. In relationships, they prioritize their accomplice's goals and emotions, making them considerate and attentive partners. However, they'll be indecisive and might want to paintings on setting boundaries to keep away from turning into overly accommodating.

Personality Number 3: Individuals with this variety will be inclined to be progressive, expressive, and outgoing. They are herbal performers who experience attention and thrive in social situations. In relationships, they'll battle with willpower or can also moreover get bored without troubles if the relationship lacks delight. Their partners need to be capable of maintain up with their power and recognize their playful nature.

Personality Number 4: People with this variety have a tendency to be practical, dependable, and hardworking. They are element-orientated and charge balance and safety. In relationships, they will be reliable and committed companions who prioritize their circle of relatives and responsibilities. However, they may war with expressing their emotions or being too rigid of their bodily activities. Their companions have that allows you to apprehend their dependability while additionally encouraging them to be more spontaneous and open.

Personality Number 5: Individuals with this variety will be inclined to be adventurous, flexible, and unconventional. They are curious and revel in exploring new research and thoughts. In relationships, they may war with willpower or may additionally furthermore end up effects bored if the connection lacks range. Their partners ought in an effort to maintain up with their spontaneity and revel in trying new matters.

Chapter 5: Numerology And Career

Finding your career course with Numerology

Numerology can be a useful tool to assist people discover their right calling and find out a pleasing profession course. By the usage of numerology, we will benefit insights into our persona inclinations, strengths, weaknesses, and herbal abilties, that may guide us in the direction of a career that aligns with our particular characteristics.

To discover your career direction with numerology, observe these steps:

Step 1: Calculate Your Life Path Number

The Life Path Number can provide perception into your innate abilities and abilities. It can also display the sort of career direction that could top notch suit you. To calculate your Life Path Number, upload up the digits of your birthdate until you get a single digit or a Master Number (11, 22, 33). For instance, in case your birthdate is October 14, 1990, your Life Path Number might be

1+zero+1+four+1+9+nine+zero = 25 = 2+five = 7.

Step 2: Determine Your Personality Number

Your Personality Number represents the way you gift your self to the world and might mean what kind of career might convey you the maximum success. To calculate your Personality Number, use the numerical fee of the consonants on your complete start name (first, middle, and final). Reduce the sum to a single digit or Master Number. For instance, if your full name is John William Smith, your Personality Number might be 1+5+1+4+9+three+four+1+nine+2+eight = 47 = 4+7 = eleven.

Step 3: Find Your Expression Number

Your Expression Number represents your natural skills and talents, which could guide you in the direction of a career that aligns collectively along side your strengths. To calculate your Expression Number, use the numerical price of the letters on your complete delivery call (first, middle, and final). Reduce the sum to a unmarried digit or Master Number. For instance, in case your whole name is John William Smith, your Expression Number is probably 1+6+8+5+5+9+1+three+4+9+2+eight = sixty one = 6+1 = 7.

Step four: Interpret Your Numbers

Now which you have your Life Path Number, Personality Number, and Expression Number, it's time to interpret what they advocate in your career course. Below are a few terrific pointers for every variety:

Life Path Number:

1: Good profession paths encompass management roles, entrepreneurship, and revolutionary fields.

2: Good career paths embody teamwork-orientated jobs, counseling, and diplomacy.

3: Good career paths encompass the humanities, leisure, writing, and verbal exchange.

4: Good career paths embody organisation, manage, and technical fields.

5: Good career paths encompass income, excursion, and unconventional art work.

6: Good career paths embody caregiving, coaching, and hospitality.

7: Good profession paths embody studies, evaluation, and academic fields.

8: Good profession paths encompass finance, regulation, and executive roles.

9: Good career paths embody humanitarian paintings, counseling, and creative fields.

Personality Number:

1: Good career paths consist of entrepreneurship, management roles, and income.

2: Good profession paths include international members of the own family, teamwork, and counseling.

3: Good career paths consist of writing, communication, and the humanities.

4: Good profession paths encompass employer, manipulate, and technical fields.

five: Good career paths encompass unconventional paintings, adventure, and profits.

6: Good profession paths embody caregiving, education, and hospitality.

7: Good profession paths include research, evaluation, and academic fields.

eight: Good career paths include finance, law, and entrepreneurship. They are inspired by using way of electricity, repute, and cloth success.

nine: Good career paths inlude humanitarian paintings, philanthropy, social justice, and the arts. They are stimulated via a choice to help others and make a powerful impact at the area. They may also moreover excel in careers associated with spirituality or recovery.

The have an impact on of Expression and Personality Numbers on career

Expression sizeable variety and profession :

Your expression variety in numerology can offer precious insights into your career route and professional aspirations. It is calculated primarily based on the letters of your full begin call, and represents your herbal abilities, abilties, and passions. Here is a manual to knowledge the career implications of each expression amount:

Expression primary:

People with an expression #1 are natural leaders and characteristic an entrepreneurial spirit. They have a sturdy stress to be successful and make an impact at the arena, and might excel in careers which consist of corporation, manipulate, politics, or regulation. They honestly have a creative aspect and might experience careers inside the arts or enjoyment corporation.

Expression amount 2:

People with an expression quantity 2 have sturdy communique capabilities and are often drawn within the direction of careers that encompass jogging with human beings, collectively with counseling, education, or social paintings. They also can excel in careers that require international own family contributors and negotiation, collectively with law or politics. They have a modern element and might additionally experience careers inside the arts or style organisation.

Expression range 3:

People with an expression variety three are innovative and function a herbal information for self-expression. They may also excel in careers inside the arts, writing, or enjoyment business company. They furthermore have notable verbal exchange competencies and might revel in careers in advertising and marketing and marketing, advertising and marketing, or public people of the family.

Expression massive range four:

People with an expression wide variety 4 are realistic and element-oriented. They excel in careers that require interest to detail, at the side of accounting, engineering, or shape. They additionally have sturdy organizational talents and might enjoy careers in control or venture control.

Expression range five:

People with an expression good sized range 5 are adventurous and revel in exploring new reviews. They may additionally excel in careers that contain journey or entrepreneurship. They surely have a innovative aspect and can revel in careers in the arts or enjoyment employer.

Expression range 6:

People with an expression quantity 6 have a natural skills for nurturing and being worried for others. They can also excel in careers in healthcare, social art work, or coaching. They additionally have sturdy organizational skills and may experience careers on top of things or undertaking control.

Expression range 7:

People with an expression variety 7 are analytical and revel in fixing complicated troubles. They might also moreover excel in careers in technological records, research, or era. They actually have a progressive thing and can experience careers within the arts or writing.

Expression extensive variety eight:

People with an expression variety 8 are herbal leaders and characteristic a robust pressure for fulfillment. They may additionally moreover furthermore excel in careers in finance, regulation, or entrepreneurship. They moreover have high-quality organizational capabilities and may revel in careers in control or project management.

Expression variety 9:

People with an expression big variety nine have a natural expertise for assisting others and creating a superb effect on the sector. They might also excel in careers in social paintings, philanthropy, or the humanities. They even have a innovative facet and may revel in careers in writing or enjoyment agency.

Personality range and profession :

In numerology, the man or woman range is calculated the usage of the consonants in a person's entire call. It represents a person's outward persona tendencies, the picture they venture to the arena, and the manner they interact with others. Understanding your character variety can offer insights into the sorts of careers that could be a precise fit for you based totally on your natural skills, strengths, and pursuits.

Personality #1: People with character number 1 are natural leaders, particularly unbiased, and self-inspired. They are driven, bold, and feature a sturdy choice to advantage fulfillment. They are tremendous trouble solvers, innovators, and considerably current people. They are incredible suitable for careers on top of things positions, entrepreneurship, earnings, and manipulate.

Personality amount 2: People with individual range 2 are as a substitute sensitive, intuitive, and diplomatic. They are herbal peacemakers and characteristic an innate ability to deliver humans collectively. They are pretty empathetic and compassionate, making them well-acceptable for careers in counseling, remedy, social paintings, and customer service.

Personality range three: People with person variety three are quite expressive, modern, and outgoing. They have incredible conversation competencies and are pretty imaginative. They are nicely-appropriate for careers in writing, appearing, music, or any career that allows them to particular themselves creatively.

Personality range 4: People with personality variety four are pretty reliable, realistic, and disciplined. They are top notch organizers and trouble solvers and thrive in based environments. They are well-ideal for careers in finance, accounting, regulation, and project management.

Personality variety 5: People with man or woman amount five are especially adaptable, adventurous, and bendy. They are commonly seeking out new evaluations and are tremendously curious about the area round them. They are properly-ideal for careers in excursion, journalism, public contributors of the circle of relatives, and any career that permits them to find out new territories.

Personality range 6: People with personality wide range 6 are exceedingly accountable, nurturing, and being concerned people. They have a sturdy choice to assist others and are relatively empathetic. They are nicely-ideal for careers in healthcare, training, counseling, or any profession that permits them to artwork with and assist others.

Personality quantity 7: People with persona amount 7 are rather intellectual, analytical, and introspective. They have awesome studies abilities and are highly curious about the area round them. They are well-appropriate for careers in technological know-how, studies, academia, and any career that requires deep questioning and assessment.

Chapter 6: Advanced Numerology

The importance of repeating numbers

Repeating numbers in numerology are the ones numbers that appear in a sequence or again and again in a person's lifestyles. These numbers have a huge impact on a person's life and are believed to keep specific messages from the universe or the spiritual realm. Here are some of the most common repeating numbers in numerology and their importance:

111: This range is regularly referred to as the "angel quantity" or the "manifestation variety." It way that your thoughts and intentions are manifesting into reality. It is a reminder to cognizance on high splendid thoughts and ideals to create the reality you preference.

222: This huge variety represents stability and concord. It is an indication which you are at the proper course and that everything is coming collectively for you. It is also a reminder to be affected man or woman and accept as true with the manner.

333: This huge variety is regularly associated with the ascended masters and represents non secular awakening and enlightenment. It is an indication which you are being guided and supported by using the usage of way of the universe and that your non secular adventure is progressing.

444: This range represents balance and basis. It is a remincer to attention for your desires and take practical steps to advantage them. It is also a sign that you are protected and supported via manner of the universe.

555: This quantity represents exchange and transformation. It is a sign that main adjustments are stepping into your lifestyles and which you need to be open to new opportunities and memories.

666: This variety is often related to negativity and fear, however in numerology, it represents balance and harmony. It is a reminder to discover stability amongst your non secular and cloth life and to release any fears or doubts which can be preserving you back.

777: This amount is regularly associated with proper accurate fortune and fortune. It represents religious awakening and enlightenment, further to inner records and intuition.

888: This amount represents abundance and prosperity. It is a sign that your difficult work and efforts are paying off and which you are being rewarded in your moves.

999: This variety represents crowning glory and endings. It is an indication that a primary financial disaster to your existence is coming to a close to and which you need to allow move of antique patterns and beliefs to make way for brand spanking new beginnings.

000: This range represents the begin of a present day cycle or adventure. It is an indication that you are starting sparkling and that the universe is supporting you in your route.

Repeating numbers can seem in hundreds of techniques, which include on license plates, mobile cellphone numbers, clocks, or even in desires. It is crucial to be privy to these symptoms and symptoms and to track into your intuition to apprehend their meaning.

For instance, if you keep seeing the variety 111, it can be a sign that you want to reputation on pleasant thoughts and beliefs to stand up your goals. If you preserve seeing the variety 444, it could be a sign which you want to stay grounded and targeted on your goals.

It is important to recall that repeating numbers are not always right or horrific, however as an alternative a mirrored image of your current mind, feelings, and actions. By tuning into the messages of repeating numbers, you can benefit perception and steerage that will help you to your adventure of private and non secular increase.

Karmic Debt Numbers

In numerology, Karmic Debt Numbers are the numbers which may be believed to have a unique spiritual significance, indicating that the individual has a few karmic lessons to have a observe on this lifetime. These numbers are regularly taken into consideration to be tough, and their impact can be felt in the direction of someone's life. The Karmic Debt Numbers include thirteen, 14, sixteen, and 19, which are derived from lowering the compound numbers to a single digit.

Karmic Debt Number thirteen: The wide variety thirteen is often associated with awful success, but in numerology, it has a deeper that means. It is associated with a lack of reputation, responsibility, and hard artwork. Those with this karmic debt quantity can also additionally discover it difficult to stay targeted and dedicated to a particular challenge or goal. They may revel in surprising changes in their existence that pressure them to conform fast.

Karmic Debt Number 14: The range 14 is associated with impulsiveness, overindulgence, and hazard-taking behavior. Those with this karmic debt range can also struggle with addictions, at the aspect of drugs, alcohol, or gambling. They can also have a tendency to be reckless and take unnecessary risks, that could bring about troubles of their non-public and professional lifestyles.

Karmic Debt Number 16: The variety 16 is associated with delight, ego, and a sense of superiority. Those with this karmic debt variety can also additionally struggle with troubles of control and manipulation. They can also moreover have a sturdy choice to be in charge and may not take kindly to being challenged or criticized. This can cause conflict of their personal and expert relationships.

Karmic Debt Number 19: The range 19 is related to self-centeredness and a loss of empathy. Those with this karmic debt significant variety might also conflict with selfishness and putting their own dreams in advance than others. They may additionally battle with communique and expressing their feelings, that would make it tough for them to form sizable relationships.

It's important to word that now not all of us with these karmic debt numbers will experience the horrible additives associated with them. It's in reality a reminder that those numbers may additionally represent areas wherein a person desires to consciousness their interest and artwork on self-improvement.

Some human beings can also moreover moreover discover that they have a couple of karmic debt numbers of their numerology chart, that can make their life path extra difficult. For example, someone with a existence route amount of 7 and a karmic debt sort of sixteen might also furthermore struggle with issues of manage and manipulation, in addition to a unethical inside the course of introspection and withdrawal.

The presence of karmic debt numbers in a person's numerology chart isn't always a awful component. It virtually approach that the person has a few crucial instructions to investigate on this lifetime. By being aware about the ones annoying situations and working to triumph over them, a person can develop and develop on a non secular level.

If you discover which you have a karmic debt massive variety on your numerology chart, it's vital to undergo in thoughts which you have the strength to alternate your existence course. By recognizing your weaknesses and operating to triumph over them, you may rework your demanding situations into possibilities for growth and self-development.

Pinnacles and Challenges

In numerology, Pinnacles and Challenges are cycles that get up inside the course of someone's life, every with their very very very own superb strength and due to this. Pinnacles are periods of time while someone studies high-quality growth and development, at the equal time as Challenges are times while someone faces limitations and struggles that need to be triumph over on the manner to hold growing.

There are 4 Pinnacles and four Challenges that someone reports during their existence, every lasting for numerous years. The particular time frame for each cycle is predicated upon on the person's Life Path Number, and may be calculated the usage of numerology.

Pinnacles:

The First Pinnacle starts offevolved at starting and lasts until the age of 27-35, relying on the man or woman's Life Path Number. This period is characterized via mastering the fundamental abilties and education critical for personal growth and development.

The Second Pinnacle lasts from the some time of 27-35 till the age of 45-fifty 3, and is a time of prolonged creativity and self-expression. This period is often marked with the aid of manner of way of the pursuit of career dreams and the improvement of private abilities.

The Third Pinnacle lasts from the some time of forty five-fifty three till the end of existence, and is a time of religious increase and self-reputation. During this period, someone is regularly interested in discover their internal self and their vicinity inside the international.

The Fourth Pinnacle takes area inside the very last years of life and represents the end quit end result of a person's existence research. This length is frequently characterized with the resource of a sense finishing touch and a focus on leaving a immoderate nice legacy.

Challenges:

The First Challenge takes location in the course of the early years of adulthood and is a time of studying and increase. This length regularly includes going through barriers and overcoming them on the way to growth greater self-self notion and self-reliance.

The Second Challenge happens in some unspecified time in the future of midlife and is a time of self-contemplated photo and evaluation. During this period, a person may also additionally revel in problems associated with relationships, profession, or personal development.

The Third Challenge happens later in existence and is a time of multiplied self-reputation and private increase. This duration frequently involves confronting one's personal fears and insecurities so you can collect more religious and emotional balance.

The Fourth Challenge takes area in the later years of lifestyles and is a time of letting flow and accepting the natural cycle of lifestyles. During this period, a person may additionally additionally additionally enjoy bodily disturbing conditions or problems associated with loss and grief.

It is essential to be conscious that while those cycles are considered great in numerology, they do now not generally dictate a person's lifestyles course. Rather, they offer a framework for data the numerous ranges of private boom and improvement that a person might also additionally experience sooner or later in their lifetime.

Example:

Let's recall an example of someone with a Life Path Number of four. The First Pinnacle for this person may closing from start till the age of 35, and is probably centered on growing sensible talents and constructing a robust foundation for non-public increase. The Second Pinnacle could rise up among the a long term of 35 and fifty 3, and might contain the pursuit of profession dreams and the development of personal competencies. The Third Pinnacle would possibly stand up from age fifty three until the stop of life, and may contain religious boom and self-popularity.

On the Challenges factor, the First Challenge for this character could arise at some point of their early years of maturity and can consist of overcoming limitations related to self-self notion and self-reliance. The Second Challenge should arise in the end of midlife and will involve personal mirrored picture and assessment, at the same time as the Third Challenge would possibly include confronting deep fears and insecurities. The Fourth Challenge ought to stand up later in life and could contain accepting the natural cycle of life and coping with troubles associated with loss and grief.

Understanding the ones cycles can provide notion and steering for personal increase and development, in addition to assist human beings navigate the numerous annoying conditions and barriers they will face for the duration of their lifetime.

Personal Year Number

In numerology, the Personal Year Number is calculated by way of the use of including the month and day of your start to the contemporary year. It is belief that this huge variety can provide belief into the problems and possibilities an extraordinary manner to get up at some point of the upcoming yr, similarly to guidance on the way to navigate them. Let's discover this idea in extra element.

To calculate your Personal Year Number, comply with these steps:

Add the digits of your shipping month and start day collectively. For instance, if you were born on June twenty seventh, you could upload 6 + 2 + 7 = 15.

Reduce this variety to a single digit via which includes the digits collectively. Continuing with the example above, 1 + five = 6.

Add the single digit to the present day 3 hundred and sixty 5 days. If the present day year is 2023, for example, you could add 6 + 2 + zero + 2 + three = 13. Then, lessen this range to a unmarried digit: 1 + three = four. Your Personal Year Number for 2023 can be four.

Now that you recognize a way to calculate your Personal Year Number, allow's find out the because of this that within the returned of every range.

Personal Year Number 1: This is a one year of latest beginnings, independence, and taking the initiative. It's a time to pursue your goals and targets with self notion, and to recollect your instincts. This three hundred and sixty five days is all about planting the seeds in your destiny fulfillment, so focus on constructing a sturdy foundation.

Personal Year Number 2: This is a year of cooperation, partnership, and international contributors of the own family. It's a time to cognizance on relationships, each non-public and professional, and to find methods to work collectively for mutual advantage. This one year is all approximately locating stability and harmony, so be affected man or woman and inclined to compromise.

Personal Year Number three: This is a year of creativity, self-expression, and socializing. It's a time to permit your hair down and have some a laugh, and to tap into your innovative side. This 12 months is all about self-development and boom, so take gain of any opportunities for studying and personal development.

Personal Year Number four: This is a 12 months of hard art work, region, and practicality. It's a time to buckle down and interest at the statistics, and to be diligent on your efforts. This yr is all about laying the inspiration for destiny success, so stay prepared and be affected character.

Personal Year Number five: This is a year of change, freedom, and adventure. It's a time to include new critiques and take dangers, and to allow skip of something this is preserving you once more. This 12 months is all about breaking unfastened from antique patterns and embracing the unknown, so be open to new possibilities and sudden twists and turns.

Chapter 7: Using Numerology In Your Daily Life

How to apply Numerology to make alternatives

Numerology is an historic tool of divination that uses numbers to gain notion into a person's individual, life path, and destiny sports. It is primarily based on the notion that each variety has a unique vibration and significance that could display hidden styles and dispositions in our lives.

While numerology isn't a era, many humans use it as a device to make selections, clear up problems, and benefit clarity about their life's motive. Here are some techniques to apply numerology in desire-making, together with actual-lifestyles examples.

Life Path Number:

One of the maximum huge numbers in numerology is the Life Path Number. It is calculated through collectively with up the digits of your transport date and lowering it to a single digit. For instance, if you have been born on August 24, 1986, your Life Path Number is probably eight+2+four+1+nine+eight+6= 38, which reduces to a few+8=eleven, and then 1+1=2. Therefore, your Life Path Number can be 2.

Your Life Path Number can display your innate abilties, strengths, and weaknesses, similarly to the possibilities and challenges you can face in life. Knowing your Life Path Number will will let you make alternatives that align together with your actual nature and cause. For instance, when you have a Life Path Number five, that is related to adventure, freedom, and trade, you may experience restless in a mundane project and might need to discover new horizons. Understanding your Life Path Number will will let you pick out a profession that permits you to express your creativity and independence.

Personal Year Number:

Another beneficial device in numerology is the Personal Year Number. It is calculated with the aid of way of along with your transport day and month to the cutting-edge 12 months and lowering it to a unmarried digit. For example, if you have been born on June 10 and the present day year is 2023, your Personal Year Number can be 6+1+0+2+zero+2+3= 14, which reduces to at least one+four=5. Therefore, your Personal Year Number for 2023 can be 5.

Your Personal Year Number can offer you with perception into the troubles and possibilities that would rise up in a particular twelve months. For instance, if you have a Personal Year Number four, this is related to difficult artwork, stability, and building foundations, you may need to consciousness for your profession, price range, and health in that three hundred and sixty five days. Understanding your Personal Year Number assist you to set desires and priorities which is probably in line with the energies of the three hundred and sixty five days.

Name Number:

In numerology, every letter of the alphabet is assigned a numerical charge, and those values are used to calculate the Name Number of a person. The Name Number can monitor your person trends, communique style, and the way others apprehend you. For instance, if your call is John Smith, your Name Number might be calculated by the usage of manner of including the numerical values of J+O+H+N+S+M+I+T+H= 1+6+8+5+1+four+nine+2+eight=forty four, which reduces to four+4=eight. Therefore, your Name Number will be eight.

Your Name Number might also have an impact in your profession selections, relationships, and success in lifestyles. For example, if you have a Name Number 1, that is associated with control, independence, and creativity, you could excel in fields that require originality and innovation, including entrepreneurship, art work, or technological understanding. Understanding your Name Number allow you to make selections approximately your profession, relationships, and private increase that align along with your innate traits.

Choosing the amazing time for crucial sports

Numerology can also be used to pick the brilliant time for important activities at the side of a marriage, beginning a brand new approach, launching a commercial organization, or signing a agreement. By aligning the power of the event with the numerological vibrations of the date and time, you could decorate the opportunities of success and harmony.

Here are a few approaches to apply numerology to pick out the extraordinary time for important sports, together with practical examples.

Numerology and Dates:

Each date has a very precise vibration and importance in numerology. To pick the super date for an occasion, you want to keep in thoughts the numerological meanings of the day, month, and 12 months.

For example, in case you are making plans to get married, you can need to select out a date that resonates with the energies of affection, harmony, and determination. A date with a Life Path Number 2 or 6 is probably exceptional, as those numbers are associated with partnerships, stability, and own family. For instance, a marriage on June 26, 2023, would in all likelihood have a Life Path Number of 6+2+6+2+0+2+3= 21, which reduces to two+1=3, quite more than a few related to creativity, delight, and celebration.

Numerology and Time:

In addition to the date, the time of the occasion also can have an impact on its very last results. Each hour of the day is associated with a planetary ruler and has a completely unique energy which could have an effect on the success of an event.

For example, in case you are launching a state-of-the-art industrial employer, you could want to select out a time that resonates with the energies of fulfillment, abundance, and growth. An auspicious time for business organisation is probably finally of the planetary hour of Jupiter, this is related to boom, prosperity, and opportunity. To locate the planetary hour of Jupiter, you need to calculate the time of sunrise and sunset in your location and divide the sunlight hours thru the use of 12. For example, if the dawn is at 6 am and the sunset is at 6 pm, the planetary hour of Jupiter is probably from eight am to nine am.

Numerology and Astrology:

Numerology and astrology are historic structures of divination that can be used collectively to pick out out the amazing time for an occasion. Each planet in astrology is related to a numerological vibration and has a specific have an effect on on specific regions of life.

For instance, in case you are signing a agreement, you can want to select a date and time that resonates with the energies of verbal exchange, clarity, and fairness. An auspicious time for contracts could be at some point of the planetary hour of Mercury, that is associated with conversation, negotiation, and contracts. To locate the planetary hour of Mercury, you need to are seeking for advice from an astrological ephemeris or a software program software application that calculates planetary hours.

Numerology and Personal Year:

Another way to choose out the first rate time for an occasion is to do not forget your Personal Year Number in numerology. Your Personal

Year Number can come up with insight into the subject matters and opportunities that could arise in a particular three hundred and sixty five days and will can help you align your dreams and priorities with the energies of the three hundred and sixty five days.

For example, in case you are starting a trendy manner, you may need to pick out a date that resonates with the energies of success, increase, and balance. An auspicious time for a modern task might be all through your Personal Year Number 8, that is associated with profession, charge variety, and authority. To locate your Personal Year Number, you want to function your starting day and month to the present day-day 12 months and decrease it to a single digit.

Creating a non-public Numerology profile

A non-public numerology profile is an fantastic manner to advantage notion into your life route, strengths, disturbing situations, and opportunities. Numerology is a divination tool that uses the vibration of numbers to show your individual, destiny, and ability. In this newsletter, we will manual you thru the way of creating a personal numerology profile and supply an motive of its key additives.

Life Path Number:

Your Life Path Number is the most critical variety in numerology and represents your widespread lifestyles motive and course. It is calculated by way of the usage of including together the digits of your start date and lowering them to a single digit or a hold close variety (eleven, 22, 33).

For instance, if you have been born on January 23, 1985, your Life Path Number may be calculated as follows:

1 + 2 + three + 1 + nine + eight + five = 29

2 + 9 = 11

Your Life Path Number is 11, a preserve near huge range related to spiritual increase, intuition, and creativity.

Expression Number:

Your Expression Number, additionally known as Destiny Number, well-known your natural skills, capabilities, and capability. It is calculated through the usage of which include collectively the digits of your entire start name and reducing them to a single digit or a hold near variety.

For example, if your complete starting call is John David Smith, your Expression Number can be calculated as follows:

1 + 6 + 8 + five + four + 1 + 4 + 9 + 4 + 1 + 4 = 47

4 + 7 = 11

Your Expression Number is eleven, the same as your Life Path Number.

Soul Urge Number:

Your Soul Urge Number, moreover known as Heart's Desire Number, famous your innermost goals, motivations, and passions. It is calculated via manner of which incorporates collectively the vowels to your entire birth name and reducing them to a unmarried digit or a draw close range.

For example, if your entire starting name is John David Smith, your Soul Urge Number might be calculated as follows:

6 + 1 + 9 + nine = 25

2 + five = 7

Your Soul Urge Number is 7, related to introspection, spirituality, and evaluation.

Personality Number:

Your Personality Number, also known as Outer Personality Number, exhibits the manner you gift yourself to the sector and the manner others understand you. It is calculated with the aid of which includes together the consonants in your whole transport call and lowering them to a unmarried digit or a master wide variety.

For instance, if your entire start name is John David Smith, your Personality Number can be calculated as follows:

1 + eight + four + 4 + 1 + four + 1 + 4 = 27

2 + 7 = nine

Your Personality Number is nine, related to compassion, idealism, and control.

Maturity Number:

Your Maturity Number reveals the classes and disturbing situations you may face for your later years and the manner you may mature and extend. It is calculated by means of way of the usage of inclusive of collectively your Life Path Number and your Expression Number and lowering them to a unmarried digit or a draw near variety.

For example, if your Life Path Number is 11 and your Expression Number is eleven, your Maturity Number might be calculated as follows:

11 + 11 = 22

Your Maturity Number is 22, a grasp range related to visionary mind, sensible competencies, and leadership.

Chapter 8: The Science Of Finding Your True Potential And Your Life Mission

Numerology: A History

Numerology, in smooth terms, refers to the studies of numbers and their this means that and effect on our each day lives. People who take into account in numerology take into account it's far a technique this is mathematically accurate in figuring out one's future, in addition to character fulfillment numbers, past lives, and plenty extra, based totally clearly at the tremendous numbers in a unmarried's every day life.

This workout called Numerology has been practiced due to the truth the dawn of arithmetic and within the sixth century the Pythagoreans are believed to were some of the first to indicate the idea that numbers have which means that inside the spiritual realm in preference to simply representing mathematical requirements. It isn't uncommon for cultures and peoples to assign a specific this means that to numbers or a selected importance Seven is concept to be fortunate for masses human beings, at the identical time as 13 is often related to lousy success. This idea is going once more millennia. Numerology virtually takes that concept and takes it one step in addition.

When operating towards Numerology, no matter the sort-which we can take a look at inside the next financial disaster-it is important to be aware that numbers are metaphysical. They are associated with the alphabet, the planets, the chakras and the Tarot, further to with crystals and music, and additionally with colorations and colorations. That is why a lot can be determined out from the check of the personal starting chart.

There are 3 essential varieties that make up Numerology, Pythagorean (or Western), Chaldean and Kabbalistic, however New Kabbalistic, Chinese and Abracadabra Numerology are also used. In the subsequent bankruptcy, we're able to examine each of these in element, the statistics in the back of them, their software, and so on. For now, it is only crucial to ensure that irrespective of which form of Numerology you pick out to work with, it is vital to stick to the high-quality shape. The versions a few of the differing types have to motive more confusion while you are trying to understand more than one, especially while you're definitely starting out.

Investigating the metaphysical nature of numbers and their vibrations.

The maximum vital numbers that Numerology examines encompass 1 through nine and The Master Numbers eleven,,, and 22. Three numbers which might be large as they advocate extra strengths and troubles. Each quantity has its own specific vibrations and energy that may be harmonious - or no longer, depending on conditions which includes track, crystal colorings, chakras, life-style alternatives, and so forth.

Vibrations are noted widespread in Chapter 6, so one may be committed to the begin date variety. Simply located, each wide range is particular and has its non-public specific vibration, much like that of each colour, gemstone or crystal, and so on.

Numerologists accept as true with that numbers are metaphysical. The metaphysical idea is that summary thoughts collectively with motive, appeared being, substance and area are a philosophical department that has its roots in truth. Because Numerology may be used to discover the big amount of statistics available, it is natural that numbers are taken into consideration metaphysical as they provide perception into the ones summary subjects.

The Benefits of Personal Numerology

Numerology gives a wealth of blessings that may be covered into your every day life. Numerology is a incredible manner to understand the character of your individual, compatibility and life-converting occasions, similarly to alternatives, and hundreds greater.

Personal Particularities

Numerology is a tremendous manner to apprehend or gain insight into your personal trends, typically through the usage of some component called a Personality Number. We'll have a check this in extra detail in Chapter 7, but for now it is enough to recognize that the Personality Number is one of the most fundamental numbers (i.E. Life Path Number or Expression Number Birth Day Number, and many others.) and well-known how different humans to start with understand you, together with the trends they count on to see.

Compatibility and Interests

Chapter 9 is dedicated to compatibility together with your partner, however this isn't the handiest kind of compatibility wherein numerology will will let you. Compatibility with particular jobs and agencies can permit humans to keep away from disappointment or losing time in a career or technique as a manner to now not be beautiful ultimately as it isn't always nicely matched with their. The Birth Number is frequently used to determine this. Your crucial numbers, specifically your Life Path Number, will can help you decide what types of sports activities you are probably to enjoy or excel in.

Life Changes

Numerology can display instances and activities which may be probably to arise internal your existence based for your non-public numerology. Using this statistics can be helpful in making prepared for the ones primary (or minor) existence activities, providing you with a extra danger of fulfillment or high nice results inside the manner. The same goes for reducing the possibilities of a few thing taking area.

Using your Life Power and Path numbers all through taking your three existence cycles and personal years, pinnacles as well as transit electricity and boundaries into interest so that you can make greater informed and higher picks about the choices you are making internal your life on the way to cause the ones most important or minor changes. As the saying is going, he who is forewarned is continuously forearmed.

Numerological Associations Colors

We referred to vibrations within the previous phase, and there are hues that align on a vibrational stage with positive numbers. Each huge variety from 1 to nine has primary and secondary sunglasses that prompt or potentiate the vibrations and developments of the amount. This list is to be had below.

Primary: crimson

Secondary: apricot, purple

Primary Orange

Secondary: salmon, gold, black

Primary: yellow

Secondary: amber, ruby

Primary: green

Secondary: brown, blue, blue, silver, indigo

Primary: blue

Secondary: cherry, crimson

Primary: indigo

Secondary: orange, mustard

Primary: violet

Secondary: magenta, pearl

Primary: purple

Secondary: ivory, opal

Primary: gold

Secondary: crimson, olive

There also are certain character characteristics for one's primary coloration:

Red: risk-taker, dominant character, visionary, passionate, lively, brave, flamboyant, tenacious.

Orange is dependable and content material cloth and is straightforward to be with, mentally and bodily properly balanced

Yellow: thrilled, realistic and self-confident. He is charming, modern, a incredible negotiator and leader, mysterious.

Green: all of the way down to earth, logical in reality, unselfish, devoted, hard to influence

Blue: optimistic, empathic and idealistic, affected person, loving, flexible and maternal.

Indigo: touchy, inquisitive, inquisitive, curious vintage soul Indigo: impulsive, formidable and curious

Violet: affectionate and cerebral antique soul, affectionate and smart romantic, creative

Rose "Pink": love, energy and management

Gold: compassion, satisfaction, information, and love.

If you've got were given ever felt interested by a selected hue on a particular day, it typically technique that the trends you are looking for are both not discovered in you or on the winning time, in any other case you want to decorate them. Therefore, you have to be privy to your emotions and get dressed for this reason because of the truth the energy and vibrations can clearly affect your day and will will let you gain dreams that you may not otherwise be capable of.

Crystal Numerology Associations

Crystals are powerful gadgets that incorporate their personal electricity, just like every residing element on Earth. Certain crystals, in addition to fine sun sun shades, are well proper with the frequencies of particular numbers, together with the large kind of the direction of life. Since crystals own bodily, emotional and highbrow talents to assist heal and offer electricity, blending them with the life route amount can produce effective results.

We will speak methods to discover your non-public lifestyles path variety in a later financial ruin. We will just list a few gems and crystals which might be related to numbers 1 through nine.

Garnet, aquamarine, obsidian, turquoise, sapphire.

Smoky quartz, rutilated quartz tourmaline, tanzanite

Amazonite, amber, amethyst, amethyst, diamond, pyrite, blue topaz

Jade, bloodstone, emerald, moonstone, black sapphire, clean quartz

Aquamarine, heliodorite, alexandrite, zincite, carnelian

Bloodstone peridot Jasper, citrine onyx, marble cat's eye, peridot

Fluorite, pearl, labradorite, rose quartz, agate

Citrine, cinnabar, ivory, opal, jet, selenite, smoky quartz

Feldspathic malachite and sandstone Yellow topaz purple and brown tourmaline Hematite, rose quartz

Numerology Tarot Associations

Tarot or tarot readings is a divinatory technique completed with a median deck of seventy eight gambling cards. Fifty six of them are called "the minor arcana", at the same time as the last 22 are referred to as "the predominant arcana". There are an countless sizable type of decks to select from. The most famous is the so-known as Ryder-Wait Tarot. These readings are finished to discover opportunities of effects, further to to assess the effect of affects affecting people, sports, or each concurrently relying on the query asked of the playing gambling cards. They are not designed to "tell the future" within the traditional enjoy. However, they'll be used to assist make picks on the same time because the route seems unsure.

The Minor Arcana

The Minor Arcana The Minor Arcana are used to recognize the bodily global. They are categorized into 4 instructions known as suits: Wands, Swords, Cups and Pentacles. Wands constitute energy of mind, Swords are associated with the thoughts, Cups correspond to emotion and Pentacles are related to fabric topics or the bodily worldwide. The gambling playing cards of those fits are numbered from 1 to ten and contain an element associated with them that is Earth, Air, Fire or Water. Wands are connected to Fire, Swords to Air, Cups to Water and Pentacles to Earth.

The 4 fits, which might be linked with their correspondences, can be used to advantage expertise and insights on particular topics. Knowing how the playing playing cards paintings when it comes to the numbers can be a excellent approach for gaining a wealth of know-how approximately oneself.

The Major Arcana

They represent vital existence events and are considered archetypal. This means that, not simplest do they've got a more significance than the fits, but moreover they have got religious importance. The 22 playing cards are numbered similarly to the in shape gambling playing playing cards, however, they may be from zero to 21. If one perspectives the playing cards as despite the fact that they had been an illustrated storybook, and reads the playing cards in order one will see the tale of a toddler's life from infancy (The Fool) to the aspect of enlightenment (The World).

The importance of numbers in the Tarot

Because every the Major and Minor Arcana are numbered, it's miles essential to remember the that means of the cardboard similarly to the amount, when you consider that five playing cards correspond to the numbers 1 through 10. While all 5 playing gambling cards are numbers

4 or four, the meanings can range drastically relying on the unique card, however it's far common that the message inside the once more of is the identical in all playing cards.

For instance, the number 1 is associated with the Ace of Pentacles, Ace of Cups, Ace of Swords, Ace of Wands and the Magician. Each of those playing cards has unique meanings, but in they all of the challenge remember of "new beginnings" is drift-reducing. It is beneficial to understand that once studying the Tarot every huge range is taken into consideration cyclical. Odd numbers recommend fluctuation and change, at the equal time as even numbers propose stability.

Below you may discover an alphabetical list of the numbers 1 through 10, as well as their meanings/institutions with the Tarot gambling cards and their this means that that with the numbers.

The best card with the zero consists of the Fool.

This card is a picture of innocence and the begin of the whole lot.

The gambling playing cards associated with the primary are: the Magician Ace of Cups, moreover called the Ace of Cups, the Ace of Spades, the Ace of Pentacles and the Ace of Wands.

Magician: The deck represents the strength of manifestat on, in addition to movements.

Ace of Cups card: Symbolizes the creative contemplating love, creativity and new relationships.

Ace of Swords: This card symbolizes intellectual clarity, fulf llment and glowing thoughts.

Ace of Pentacles The Ace of Pentacles is a image of the possibility of a latest career route (career-sensible, in addition to financially) prosperity, abundance and manifestation.

Ace of Wands: This card is a picture of new possibilities, potential and the capability to inspire.

The playing cards bearing the range 2 are the High Priestess and the Two of Cups, the Two of

Swords, the Two of Pentacles and the Two of Wands.

The High Priestess card symbolizes sacred statistics, instinct and the divine woman.

The Two of Cups card symbolizes relationships, mutual attraction and unifying love.

The Two of Swords: The card symbolizes the need for avoidance, making difficult alternatives and weighing numerous alternatives.

The Two of Pentacles symbolizes time control, flexibility and loads of priorities.

The Two of Clubs card symbolizes the future, selections and the device of discovery.

Cards which is probably associated with the variety 3 include the Empress Three of Cups, the Three of Cups, the Three of Swords, the Three of Pentacles and the Three of Wands.

The Empress card: A image of splendor and abundance, the girl and the natural worldwide.

The Three of Cups: This card symbolizes collaboration, friendship, birthday celebration and innovative wondering.

The Three of Swords. This card symbolizes the feelings of grief, emotional pain, disappointment and sorrow.

The Three of Swords deck symbolizes collaboration, teamwork and execution.

Three of Wands: This card is a photograph of growing development, growth and the capacity to see in advance.

The playing cards that are related to the extensive range four are the Emperor, the Four of Cups, the Four of Swords, the Four of Pentacles and the Four of Wands.

The Emperor card symbolizes authority, status quo and form.

The Four of Cups symbolizes reflected image, re-assessment and meditation.

Four of Swords The Four of Swords card symbolizes rest, meditation and relaxation.

The Four of Pentacles card symbolizes manipulate, safety and conservatism.

The Four of Clubs: The card is a image of homecoming, satisfaction and party.

Cards which can be related to the numbers 5 encompass the Hierophant The Hierophant, the Five of Cups, the Five of Swords, the Five of Pentacles and the Five of Clubs.

The Hierophant card is a image of non secular information, way of life and conformity.

Five of Cups: Symbolizes remorse, sadness and pessimism.

Five of Swords: The card symbolizes conflict, war of phrases and even defeat.

Five of Pentacles: The symbolizes poverty, economic loss and loneliness.

Five of Clubs (additionally called the Five of Wands): This deck represents variations, variety and tension.

Cards bearing the huge variety 6 embody the Lover of Cups, the Six of Cups, the Six of

Swords, the Six of Pentacles and the Six of Wands.

The Lover: It is a card that represents harmony in relationships, options and love.

The Six of Cups card is a image of nostalgia for early life, love and innocence.

The Seven of Swords: This card symbolizes changes, transitions, an act of passage.

The Six of Pentacles symbolizes generosity, giving in addition to sharing cash.

Seven of Clubs: The card symbolizes public recognition, self-self notion and the possibility of success.

The playing cards which can be associated with the 7 are the Seven of Seven, the Seven of Cups, the Seven of Swords, the Seven of Pentacles and the Seven of Wands.

The Chariot: It is a picture of strength of mind, strength of will and manipulate.

The Seven of Cups is a symbol of possibilities, options and phantasm.

Seven of Swords This card is a photo of deception and betrayal.

The Seven of Pentacles deck symbolizes lasting consequences, funding and persistence.

Seven of Wands This card symbolizes the concept of venture, competition and additionally protection.

Cards which may be related to the quantity eight embody Strength and the Eight of Cups, the Eight of Swords, the Eight of Pentacles and the Eight of Clubs.

It is a card of energy that may be a photograph of effect, strength, in addition to persuasion.

The Eight of Cups card symbolizes loss and displeasure.

The Eight of Swords card symbolizes negativity and victimization.

8 of Pentacles: The image symbolizes mastery, repetitive responsibilities and expertise development.

The Eight of Clubs card symbolizes alignment, movement and the capability to move.

Cards which can be related to the numbers nine encompass the Hermit Nine of Cups, The Nine of Cups, the Nine of Swords and the Nine of Pentacles, and the Nine of Wands.

The Hermit The Hermit: This card symbolizes the soul's search for introspection, soul looking and internal guidance.

The Nine of Cups: Symbolizes gratitude and happiness.

Nine of Swords The Nine of Swords card symbolizes melancholy, anxiety and worry. Tension. Tension.

Nine of Pentacles: The deck symbolizes monetary freedom, similarly to pricey and wealth.

Nine of Clubs: The symbolizes limits, braveness, in addition to the potential to conquer.

The gambling gambling cards that correspond to the variety 10 are the Wheel of Fortune, the

Ten of Cups, the Ten of Swords, the Ten of Pentacles and the Ten of Wands.

The Wheel of Fortune: This card symbolizes destiny, karma and the cycles of existence.

The Ten of Cups: This card is a photograph of divine love, harmony and alignment.

Ten of Swords: This card is a picture of an unsettling finishing, loss or crisis.

Ten of Pentacles: The is a symbol of contributing financial protection, and wealth.

10 of Clubs: The card symbolizes the very last contact of a assignment, burden, and difficult art work.

The final four gambling playing cards that aren't numbered consist of Pages, Knights, Queens similarly to Kings in every of the suits. These Major Arcana playing cards, 11 via 21, may be decreased to unmarried digit numbers as they've a similar meaning and simplify matters.

Numerology and Music Connections

You won't make sure how track and numbers paintings together, but they do. Many well-known composers you've got were given encountered have combined music and numbers.

Some of Plato's manuscripts are even believed to incorporate mathematical symbolism for musico-mathematical use. Plato carried out this through dividing an octave into twelve tones. After dividing his complete textual content into 12 it become located that there had been "splendid principles" that have been associated with the intervals of the Pythagorean scale, that have been harmonious, similarly to dissonant periods that contained negative standards.

You can be wondering why this became so critical and the solution is pretty easy. Plato concept that the complete worldwide became controlled thru numbers and not thru the gods, which brought on him to provoke Pythagorean Numerology. In the length of Plato's life and in keeping with the Greeks his art work turn out to be to be categorised as medical, musical arcana. This modified into critical because it implied that more which means may be decided in his writings if one modified into capable of decipher their because of this that.

Famous composers which incorporates Schumann, Bach, Schoenberg, Peter Maxwell Davies, Berg and loads of different musicians have covered numbers into their track. Many even used mysterious numbers to carry their deeper musical which means.

Numerological Organizations Planets in Astrology

Astrology is the concept that you could studies statistics thru studying the movements of the planets and their positions, in particular those who befell at the time and date you were born (if they're associated with you, then obviously). In smooth terms, Astrology is the study of the motion of the planets and their orbits, however, as with Numerology there are various factors to this approach.

The Sun affects identity and life. The Moon affects protection and emotions, Mercury influences communique and the thoughts,

Venus affects relationships and choice. Mars influences motion and motivation, Jupiter influences abundance and nicely fortune, Saturn affects boundaries and training. Uranus affects trade and rise up, Neptune impacts creativeness and optimism, and Pluto impacts transformation and energy.

Your Zodiac signal is the only that determines your number ore tendencies, furthermore known as your Sun sign, but this doesn't mean that it's far the handiest Zodiac sign you may find out on your Astrology chart. We are all an amalgamation of numerous Zodiacs, and planets dwelling in one among a type Houses, which has a one-of-a-type have an impact on on us.

The most popular numbers in Astrology are 1 through 9. There are 9 planets which is probably part of our sun system, each of which corresponds to as a minimum one or greater of the numbers. People born on particular dates are ruled via nice zodiacs and planets. The 9 digits will ring a bell, as they're the important numbers appreciably utilized in Numerology.

One of the maximum essential

The Sun

Birthday of any month: 28 19 10 and 1

Ruler of the Leo planets

Two

The Moon

Birthday of any month: 29 20 11 and a couple of.

The planetary ruler of Cancer

Three.

Jupiter

Birthday of any month: 30 21 12 and three.

The Planetary Ruler of Sagittarius and Pisces

Number four

Uranus

Birthdays of any month: 31, 22 thirteen, and four.

Five.

Mercury

Birthdays of any month: 23, 14, and 5.

The planetary ruler of Virgo and Gemini.

Sixth huge range

Venus

Birthdays of any month: 24 6, 15 and 24

The Planetary Ruler of Libra and Taurus

Seventh range

Neptune

Birthdays of any month: 25 or sixteen, and seven.

Planetary ruler of Cancer

Number 8

Saturn

Birthdays of any month: 26, 17, and eight.

The planetary ruler of Aquarius, Capricorn and Libra

Number 9

Mars

Birthdays of any month: 27, 18 and 9

The Planetary Ruler of Scorpio and Aires

Both Astrology and Numerology are intrinsically related, as many calculations are used to observe your astrological chart, plus numbers are determined in nearly each trouble of our lives.

Chapter 9: "The Universal Truth Of Numbers

In Chapter 1, there are numerous sorts of Numerology. In this financial disaster, we will take a look at the super bureaucracy, starting with the 3 crucial types.

Western or Pythagorean Numerology

This form of Numerology is the notable acknowledged and maximum widely used. It became superior by manner of the usage of the Greek metaphysician, astrologer, musician and mathematician Pythagoras, who lived within the sixth century. It is not clean if Pythagoras modified into the right writer of Numerology or if he have become great one of the first to apply it and unfold its teachings to his students. However, the fact remains that he used Numerology to expect future events and the destiny of these who have been divine and lots more.

Pythagoras believed that every planet turn out to be related to a selected sound and become represented via precise numbers. He believed that classifications in conjunction with introverted or extroverted individual lovely, ugly, or unpleasant are elements from which it changed into viable to provide an cause for the numbers.

The technique of using Pythagorean numerology consists of assigning 9 vital numbers (1 to nine) to the Greek alphabet. The Pythagoreans remember that the numbers repeat themselves. When the variety 10 is reached, 1 is extended thru 0 to reach at 1. This is the same for any quantity that is a composite (other than any of the maintain near numbers) thinking about they could all be reduced to a unmarried digit range.

The meanings of the easy numbers of Pythagorean Numerology are explained beneath.

Creation

Omniscient

Creativity

Stability and resilience

Unpredictable, active, dynamic

Mothering, being concerned

Looking, wondering

Balance, power

Idealism this is the principle of life.

In the Pythagorean form of Numerology there are styles of frequencies which can be essential and draw near. The numbers 1 thru 9 include smooth vibrations, like a few other -digit quantity that may be reduced to a single-digit huge range. There are two numbers of draw near vibrations: eleven, and 22, which do no longer combine to make a single digit range. These hold close numbers symbolize the Karma that determines a person's fulfillment or failure of their modern-day state of affairs. Both hold close and basic numbers are characterised through immoderate great and horrible elements as the entirety in life.

In addition to the grasp numbers there also are karmic debt numbers - 19, sixteen, 14 and 13. In the words of Pythagoras and his enthusiasts, the ones numbers mirror the outcomes of previous lives which have been so terrible that they created a karmic debt that carried over to the following. Karmic numbers are explored in more intensity in Chapter 7, while we study the frequency their names deliver. It is normal to apply each the date of delivery and your name to decide the which means of Western Numerology, and as with Chaldean and Chaldean, which we're capable of discover in addition in the chapter we speak the hyperlinks amongst these numbers.

As with the karmic debt quantity, every large range has absolutely and negatively charged electricity associated with it. This is essential to keep in mind as people regularly wonder if they're like minded with a companion, family member, buddy or possibly colleagues. While studying the numbers it's miles important to keep every sides in mind. Even at the equal time as human beings's life numbers look like similar, there may be a possibility that they may now not in shape. This is because of the fact that one might be bringing negative energies into the numerology of the alternative. In order for this no longer to arise, it is critical to apprehend the expectation one has of the companion.

Pythagorean Numerology makes use of elements which consist of the soul impulse range, life path vast range, private numbers, Pythagorean Arrows, names, expression numbers, in addition to a adulthood variety, to decide the future of an man or woman. We will move over all of those factors in more detail inside the path of this e-book, in addition to educate you on a way to perceive every of these numbers for yourself!

At this thing all you want to maintain in thoughts is the reality that the idea of Pythagorean Numerology starts with 6 important numbers: three out of your infant's name and three from your birthday. These six numbers are called the six vibrations. They are the variety that represents your life route The birthday range the extensive shape of the number one effect the quantity of the internal soul or vowels, the type of the characters or consonants, similarly in your numbers of expression.

Kabbalah Numerology

This is the form of Numerology this is usually employed at the equal time as reading names and is form of as nicely known as the Western Numerology of Pythagoras. Kabbalah Numerology originated with Hebrew mysticism. It modified into based on the use of the Hebrew alphabet and its 22 vibrations to useful aid in divining records. It have come to be later modified into Greek, in addition to the Roman alphabets, as well.

The 10 one-of-a-type strength resources applied in Kabbalah calculations are Malkuth, Yesod, Hod, Netzach, Taphareth, Geburah, Chesed, Binah, Chokhmah and Kether.

The word originates from the 13th century Kabbalists, who believed that the Old Testament become a secret code ordained thru way of God and used Numerology to clear up it, finally the call Kabbalah Numerology. It is concept that Kabbalah moreover achieved an critical feature in occultism along with Tarot studying. Incredibly, there are 22 letters inside the Hebrew alphabet, and there are 22 Major

Arcana playing playing cards, and it's far believed that they join and provide a greater records of every distinct, due to the truth each of the 22 Major Arcana gambling gambling playing cards are specially identified by way of way of numbers.

Other forms of Numerology collectively with Pythagorean and Chaldean, for instance, you need to recognise not simplest your call, but additionally the date of delivery, time of start and so forth. For Kabbalah Numerology all this is required is the character's call. It is obviously much less difficult, but, it leads a few practitioners to don't forget that it isn't surely powerful, because it does now not provide the identical depth of information, due to the reality you're simplest extracting facts from the man or woman's name. There are some vital statistics that the date of delivery, time or superb information. Can display, or even without the more numbers, we aren't able to get admission to the extra facts.

Like Pythagorean Numerology, each letter of the alphabet is attached to a selected range.

However, those numbers exceptional help to determine an preliminary numerical charge. Kabbalah has over 4 hundred course numbers, which makes it difficult to come to be aware about the right Kabbalah range for someone if one makes a decision to examine all viable paths. Many favor to deal with the numbers which may be commonplace to this purpose.

To determine your Kabbalah huge variety, you need to

Translate the letters of your personal name (first, middle and very last name are included) the usage of the Hebrew translation alphabet.

1. A, J, S

2. B K T

three. C 3: C, L and U

4: D 4, M four: D, M

5 five: W, E and W

6 6. F, O 6: F, O

7: G P, G, Y

eight Z: H, Q, Z

9 I nine, R

All numbers

Divide this general via way of nine

Add 1 to the give up cease result of the previous step: this range can be your personal Kabbalah variety.

Let's look at an instance. Let's say your name is added to 40 4. Then you may do the subsequent:

40 4 / 9 = 4.Eight

eight. The the rest.

$8 + 1 = 9$

The quantity 9 represents your Kabbalah tremendous range.

When you have got were given pretty a number of similarly divisible with the aid of 9, for example, 36, then you could definitely view the extensive variety as 36.Zero Add 1 to zero and if you need to come up with a Kabbalah range of 1.

Kabbalah numbers from 1 to 9, and the meanings they convey.

Development

Increase

Affection

Uselessness

Genesis

Implementation

Mysticism

Impulsiveness

Luck

While the different sorts that make up Numerology translate their alphabets into numerical numbers however do no longer translate in the same manner further to the identical alphabet/amount suit. In Pythagorean Numerology, it's miles mentioned that in conjunction with the 9 moreover disregards all information after the 8 letters or numbers.

New Kabbalistic Numerology

This specific shape this is part of Kabbalah Numerology changed into derived from the Roman alphabet interpretation. Like the unique version used, this one is based mostly on one's name in choice to birthday and employs Pythagorean strategies to calculate the dates. This is because the New Kabbalah Numerology focuses extra on the life activities of the character's tendencies.

Luria advanced a theosophical framework that, in line with his fanatics, fostered an financial belief tool of dialogue, belief and critique that, at the same time, presented a whole description of humanity's role inside the global community in a way that is morally, spiritually and intellectually important to us. This triggered the introduction of the New Kabbalah.

The purpose of the New Kabbalah is to growth or decorate the philosophical and mental meaning of symbols and mind which may be basically Kabbalistic. Unlike many different kinds of Numerology which is probably used, the New Kabbalah makes use of a mix of Hinduism, Platonism, Buddhism, Gnosticism and Jewish mysticism, which permits this form to be greater encompassing than traditional Kabbalah Numerology.

The location of its New Kabbalah variety is same to the actual version, the only distinction being that it is considered in conjunction thru the usage of the mental and philosophical practices cited above.

Chaldean Numerology

Chaldean Numerology, it is regularly known as Mystical Numerology is carefully related with Astrology as it is derived from Mesopotamia The area that became the start for Western Astrology. This shape of Numerology is also associated with the Kabbalah in addition to the Indian Vedic device. It is thought to be a greater correct version than Pythagorean Numerology. However, it's miles lots an awful lot less broadly recognized because of its hassle.

This form of Numerology makes use of a device that is tough for masses to apprehend or even draw near. The values assigned to the alphabet aren't systematic as they're for Pythagorean Numerology further to Kabbalah. Chaldean Numerology is often known as mystical numerology because of the fact that it makes a speciality of the occult and metaphysical elements of 1's person and future. In clean phrases, this shape of Numerology is used to discover forces invisible to the naked eye, which could have an effect on someone's existence.

The Chaldean humans invented this sort of Numerology and function contributed substantially to mathematics, Numerology, Astrology and plenty of various fields of check due to their good sized study.

Chaldean Numerology is super from wonderful kinds of Numerology for some one-of-a-kind motives. The first is that the decision the character makes use of to bet isn't usually the call he or she end up born with or the call thru which she or he is first rate recognised. Another distinction is that their substantial range system is based totally mostly on 1-eight rather than 1-9. This is due to the reality nine is considered a sacred variety. It is one of the most sacred numbers in recent times. The only case in which the range 9 is used is whilst your call is a nine. This implies that the letters assigned to each number variety from the letters used for Kabbalah and Pythagorean Numerology.

According to the Chaldean Numerology System, the numbers are represented thru the letters in the following order.

1 A, I, J Q 1: A, I, J, Q

2 2: B 2, K R

three. C 3, G 3, S

four. D 4, M and T

5. E five: E, H, N 5, X

6. U, V, W

7. O, Z

eight. F, P

Chaldean Numerology makes use of the person's date of start and believes it's far the second maximum massive element of its research. It moreover includes including up the numbers that make up the decision of 1's desire. The this means that of each range is exactly similar to in Pythagorean Numerology. However, in Chaldea multiple large form of 1 digit is used. It is important to recognise the way to judge any compound large range, as they're a photograph of the metaphysical and/or deeper because of this behind the call.

These numbers are obtained thru together with 3 (or if the individual does not have a center name) digits of each call, without reducing them to single numbers. Once you've got the single digit and composite numbers, it's time to consist of the date of starting within the system.

Suppose, as an instance, that the person for whom we are acting a Chaldean reading is Ann Marie Jones, and that she become born on June 2, 1984.

First, decide the tool for figuring out the names starting with the letters "1, the center call and the numbers of the final name.

First call First name: 1+5 + five = eleven.

Middle call Middle call 2 , 1 + five, equals 13.

Last name Last name: 1 + 7 + five + + + three = 21

Step 2: Reduce each range to at least one digit, however be conscious the quantity of composite numbers to decide the call.

First call First call: 1 . + 1 equals 2.

Middle call 1 + three =

Last call Last name: 2 + 1 = three

Step three: Add the three collectively.

2 + 4 + three= 9

Step 4: Determine your date of begin. For example, June 2, 1984, that is 06/02/1984.

zero + 6 + zero + 2 + 1 + nine + 8 + four = 30

Step 5: Reduce the amount of digits to at least one.

3 + zero = three

Once you have got got were given all of the vital numbers and information, you could study their frequency. It is possible to decide the distinction among your name and your whole name has awful or incredible vibrations. Single digit numbers imply how others understand your appearance. All numbers are searching out recommendation from additives or affects that aren't visible, that could play an important position on your existence, that you couldn't be privy to, or in sure instances provide clues or predictions for the destiny.

It is important to recall that every composite massive variety has a fantastic because of this based totally on its roots (1 from 1 to nine), further to the numbers 10 to fifty two have a honest deeper and extra particular which means. Most humans stay with fifty because of the reality it is the 52nd week of the 365 days There isn't any need for maximum humans to transport any further.

Here is the correspondence of each range constant with Chaldean Numerology.

Self-sufficient and dominant

Adaptability and compatibility

Creativity

Discipline

Freedom, journey

Active, enthusiastic

Curiosity

Ambition, self-control

Helpful, compassionate

Greater opportunity of reaching honor

Dangers of life

Anxiety and ache

Power and exchange

Financial and/or business organisation success

Favorable even as paired with a pleasing fee, in any other case negative.

Be extremely careful whilst making an essential or huge selection

Lucky if related to an 8 or a 4.

Life is complete of dangers.

Success, achievement, happiness

Waiting, problem in getting the arena

Honor, fulfillment and achievement

Late actions, threat

High success charge, real fortune

Long existence, affection, assist

Trials that result in fulfillment

Fear of these round you

Authority, power, intelligence

Danger of lack of lifestyles, pain

Unexpected danger, deception, trials

Neutral variety that has the capacity to obtain success

General

Best if decided with the aid of intuition

Love, useful resource, affection

Work hard and you will be successful

Fear

Power, authority as 27

Love, coins, friendship

Mistrust, danger, uncertainties

The first-class manner to get power is through strolling difficult

General wide range

The key to success is to pay interest in your inner voice in preference to counting on others

Love, affection and assist Similar to 24 hours of affection, affection and aid.

Unfortunate sports, screw ups, losses.

Risk of these near you

Power and authority are without hassle handy

Love, friendship and cloth achievement

Deception, grief - are like 40 4

Neutral variety, success proportional to the quantity of exertions finished

Loneliness, isolation

The key to achievement is to apply your instinct and now not the advice of the bulk

The fulfillment of being a leader

Financial loss, failure unfortunate life outcomes

It is not realistic to look at the Chaldean Numerology device in a single day, however, in case you select to have a take a look at this shape similarly, you may benefit many blessings.

Chinese Numerology

This is the first version of Numerology that we are capable of see that has a records due to the fact the story of its delivery. Legend has it that the Emperor of China Emperor Yu have become able to see an animal shell with a grid of 9 squares that turn out to be perfectly uniform, and brought into consideration it to be a magic rectangular. Because the turtle changed into determined within the Lo River and the grid changed into named Lo Shu Square/ Grid. Lo Shu Square/ Grid. The historic Chinese believed, a few 4000 years within the beyond, that range end up at the base of all matters.

The reason of this grid is to multiply numbers vertically, horizontally or diagonally to create 15. This variety come to be chosen due to the reality it is the precise massive fashion of days among the contemporary moon day and the whole moon day. The grid can be used to assess someone's strengths and developments close to their destiny improvement.

To use the grid, the month of begin is needed on the facet of the three hundred and sixty five days of shipping and date of delivery to determine that man or woman's traits. It is essential to do away with the zeros and simplest the numbers 1 via nine are used. For example, if your birthday fell on July 5, 1983, you will write it as 7/five/1983, in vicinity of 07/05/1983.

The frequency with which the equal variety seems in the three hundred and sixty 5 days of starting moreover determines the person traits of a particular individual. The listing may be as follows.

1.

Occurs as soon as: introvert

2. Occurs two times: communicative

Occurs 3 times: talkative

3. Occurs 4 instances: 4 times Affectionate

Number 2

Occurs once: sensitive

Occurs instances: colourful

Occurs 3 times: extremely touchy

Occurs four instances: lonely

3.

Occurs as quickly as: incredible

Occurs twice: innovative

Occurs 3 instances: modern

Occurs 4 times: overly resourceful

4.

Occurs as soon as: solid and orderly

Occurs two times: pragmatic

Occurs 3 times: hard-working

Occurs 4 times: bodily exercising

5

Occurs as quickly as: affectionate

Occurs instances: continual

Occurs 3 times Determined

Four times: instantaneous actions

6.

Once is a exceptional time to are seeking out recommendation from

Occurs twice: originating

Occurs three times: warm Temperate

Occurs four times: emotional

Number 7

Occurs once: analyzing reviews

Occurs two times: religious

Occurs 3 instances: inclination to loss

Occurs four instances: life issues

Number 8

Occurs once: meticulous

Occurs instances: rigid

Occurs three times: materialistic Materialistic

Occurs 4 instances: continuously at the bypass

Number 9

Occurs as soon as: practical

Occurs twice: crucial

Occurs three times: Givers

Occurs four times: superb, however lonely

The way to interpret the rows is as follows:

The top row of horizontals revolves spherical cerebral thinking, accurate judgment and reasoning, and creativeness.

The center row specializes in emotions and emotions, which embody instinct and spirituality.

The backside horizontal row specializes in athletic ability, practicality and not unusual experience, similarly to precise bodily elements.

The vertical row A specializes in motion and gadgets things in motion.

The middle vertical row revolves round achievement, strength of mind and perseverance.

The left vertical row makes a speciality of the capacity to anticipate creatively, in addition to intellectual capacity and the functionality to understand mind.

Since each Astrology and Numerology are so carefully interconnected, it is not sudden that Chinese Numerology makes use of Astrology's rationalization of the five elements, Earth, Water, Fire, Metal and Wood. Each of the elements has its very own set of institutions which can be useful in retaining the zodiac picture in thoughts whilst performing this type of numerology.

Earth: 8, five, 2

Fire: nine

Water: 1

Metal: 7, 6

Wood: 4, 3

To location your numbers at the grid, examine those suggestions:

The massive range nine is typically positioned inside the better proper corner.

The variety 8 seems in the center of the proper aspect.

The variety 7 constantly appears at the bottom of the right aspect.

The big range 6 normally seems on the top of the middle field.

five. The variety 5 appears within the center.

The massive range 4 continuously seems located in the middle of the decrease square.

The amount three continuously appears in the pinnacle a part of the left aspect.

The amount 2 continually seems inside the middle of the left factor.

The no 1 typically seems at the bottom of the left difficulty.

If you have got have been given more than of the identical amount, then you may region they all in the real rectangular. For example, in case you have been born on June 6, you can placed the two 6's in the top center rectangular. By interpreting the above numbers and rows, you may be able to determine your inclinations (or those of whomever the grid is for).

One component to preserve in mind is that there can be a difference many of the Western and Eastern interpretation of the numbers. You can pick out out both one to set your grid based totally on which one you experience extra connected to. Because the Lo Shu grid is the Lo Shu grid can be described as heavily inspired with the aid of using manner of Eastern way of life you could favor to stick with the Eastern interpretations, but it isn't always vital.

Below is an evaluation of the Eastern and Western interpretations of each variety, and their terrible traits.

Number One

Eastern: ethical, unbiased in their approach, and in a position to overcome boundaries.

Western: powerful, leaders, bosses, achievers, achievers.

Negatives: easy to end up aggressive or irritated

Number Two

Eastern: determination, good fortune

Western: unstoppable, effective, calm, diplomatic, mild persuasion

Positives: low vanity, excessive jealousy

Three

Eastern: abundance, increase

Western: colourful, cheerful, social, tremendous, extraordinary

Negative elements: scatterbrained, selfish

Fourth huge range

Eastern: struggles, issues

Western: dependable and tough-operating, satisfied with the existence of a simple man

Negative elements: closed-minded, without issue upset and decided to move their very personal manner.

Five

Easterners The time period "Eastern" can advise immoderate first-rate or terrible, or stability.

Westerners are socially extroverted, lively, energetic.

Negative factors: inconsistent, risky and addictive.

Sixth Number

Eastern: abundance, coins

Westerners are compassionate, loving and sort. Peaceful, nurturing

Negative elements embody emotional guilt

Number Seven

Oriental: social, human beings abilities, relational abilities

Western Spiritual, charming, charming Deep philosopher, fascinating

Negative additives: withdrawn of their thoughts

Number Eight

Oriental Wealth, abundance True fortunate quantity

Western: abundance, pleasure, energy, intelligence

Negative elements: unwillingness to provide, greed for money

Number Nine

Eastern Luck, happiness and prolonged life

Western A combination of excellent traits, fascinating, progressive and affected individual.

Negative factors: realize-it-all and insecure.

Abracadabra Numerology

This is the a high-quality deal much less famous shape of Numerology that employs triangles to calculate numbers describing characters and events the usage of the person's initial phrase. The values of the variety given to the word Abracadabra correspond to 365, because of this that it covers the entire year.

The triangles used on this shape of numerology have their basis in Giza, Egypt, within the brilliant pyramids that have been built at Cheops. There is a perception that those historical pyramids held historic secrets and techniques and techniques and strategies, and this Inverted Triangle (or pyramid) is the idea of this technique. The base of the triangle is the 9 letters of the call, and or their numerical equivalents.

Abracadabra Numerology is a mysterious and mystical device that well-known the foundation amount of a person's delivery call and lets in you to turn out to be aware of the developments that symbolize her or him. The alphabetical translation of all Abracadabra Numerology numbers is to be had under.

A, J, S

B, K, T

C, L, U

D M V

E, N, W

F O, F, O

G P, Y

H, Q Z

I R

They need to be much like diverse types of Numerology that we have mentioned in the preceding sections. The high-quality manner to maintain from this factor is to create tables displaying the values of every letter. This lets in you to look it up without trouble.

To begin, type to your preliminary call. Then, below every phrase, you ought to write the numbers from the tables or from the list above. Start along with the numbers on every line via manner of putting them 2 through way of two simply so every descending line has one a awesome deal less extensive range than the street earlier than it. All compound numbers must be decreased to unmarried digits within the same way as we have been doing for maximum amazing kinds of Numerology. The only difficulty to do is to combine the two numbers. From this point on, you have to join all of the single digit composite digits into strains, just like the manner you probable did at the beginning. Each descending line has one much less quantity than the preceding one. Keep in conjunction with till there are unmarried-digit numbers at the give up in the triangle (the "dot"). The very last extensive variety is your Abracadabra wide range.

Let's do an example collectively. Let's say the problem's name might be Ana. Here are the steps vital to find Anna's Abracadabra massive variety.

A n n

1 5 five 1

6 6

12

3

The first aspect we do is print Ana's name.

Next, we write the numbers much like each letter.

Then we add them in agencies.

1 + 5, five + 1.

We have 6 and 6 inside the next row.

On the opportunity aspect, we upload six and six which offers us 12 for the subsequent row.

There isn't any way to get a -digit amount, so we need to feature 1 + 2.

We are left with the Abracadabra quantity of 3.

You can be thinking about what to do when you have names that don't include a remarkable style of letters, so allow's installation an example for this situation as well. Let's consider that our hassle call turn out to be Tiffany.

Chapter 10: Discover Who You Are Purported To Be A Step-Thru-Step Guide.

The natal chart, every now and then called the begin chart is best a cool lively movie of the sky, take into account yourself because the Moon, Sun, asteroids and planets at the proper 2d you have got been born. According to astrologers and numerologists, the shipping chart is the underlying outline of the life you've got lived. It gives precise insight into your man or woman weaknesses, in addition for your strengths, conduct, dislikes, goals and lots more.

Your start chart famous your moon sign, solar symptoms, growing and falling sign, your houses, as well as the region of the planets inside the direction of your beginning, similarly to the house in which you resided. It may also additionally provide a wonderful deal of data as to why you act the manner you do, or keep in mind topics the manner you do or expect the manner you do, and so forth. The element to maintain in mind is that not all thoughts are going to resonate with you, this is perfectly everyday! Consider what you need and overlook approximately the rest.

Using an astrological tracker, or a calculator available on net web sites, is the maximum accessible technique of obtaining your beginning chart. And it's miles normally free! There are many varieties of charts that serve extremely good features. In this manual, we are able to consciousness on circle charts. The number one advantage is that those net sites provide a entire description and breakdown of the complete chart, so that you do not want to do any guesswork. Of direction, it is without a doubt beneficial to drill down into regions you're unsure or unsure about, but for the most element on line calculators excel at explaining the whole chart in a single vicinity.

All you want to understand to get entry to your shipping chart to your phone or computer are the subsequent facts about your personal data:

Date of beginning

Month of shipping

Year of start

State of beginning

Place of delivery metropolis

Hour of starting

Minute of start

The motive it need to be correct is the truth that everything is in motion, due to this that stars, planets and all things can alternate inside the span of an hour. This ought to drastically adjust your infant's start chart.

It is vital not to be compelled with the natal chart with the resource of way of the Life Path Numbers, Soul Impulse numbers or another records. This statistics is probably revealed later and could play into the start chart, however they're now not the primary information of the beginning chart. We is probably capable of discover all of our number one numbers in later chapters.

It is likewise critical to pick out which residence device you pick out to rent Although there are numerous options to be had, those are the most famous: Koch, Placidus and complete signs and symptoms. In this manual, we can address Placidus due to the reality they produce an easy-to-comply with, newbie-excellent chart.

After charting on-line (take into account to pick out the spherical chart as it's far the very best to understand) you could get a image of your natal chart. Below that pictograph, you may get in-depth elements for every phase of your chart, typically beginning with the solar sign.

www.ingramcontent.com/pod-product-compliance
Lightning Source LLC
Chambersburg PA
CBHW071445080526
44587CB00014B/1995